AF559637

RESILIENT INDIA

RESILIENT INDIA

How Modi Transformed India's Disaster Management Paradigm

Edited and compiled by: BlueKraft Digital Foundation
Research by: Modi Story

RUPA

Published by
Rupa Publications India Pvt. Ltd 2023
7/16, Ansari Road, Daryaganj
New Delhi 110002

Sales centres:

Bengaluru Chennai Hyderabad
Jaipur Kathmandu Kolkata
Mumbai Prayagraj

Copyright © BlueKraft Digital Foundation 2023

The views and opinions expressed in this book are the author's own and the facts are as reported by them which have been verified to the extent possible, and the publishers are not in any way liable for the same.

All rights reserved.
No part of this publication may be reproduced, transmitted, or stored in a retrieval system, in any form or by any means, electronic, mechanical, photocopying, recording or otherwise, without the prior permission of the publisher.

P-ISBN: 978-93-5702-957-5
E-ISBN: 978-93-5702-917-9

First impression 2023

10 9 8 7 6 5 4 3 2 1

The moral right of the author has been asserted.

Printed in India

This book is sold subject to the condition that it shall not, by way of trade or otherwise, be lent, resold, hired out, or otherwise circulated, without the publisher's prior consent, in any form of binding or cover other than that in which it is published.

Contents

Introduction / vii

Chapter 1
The Tears of Morbi 1979 / 1

Chapter 2
Devastation in Kutch / 22

Chapter 3
Kutch Bounces Back / 42

Chapter 4
Mission Preparedness / 68

Chapter 5
The Making of a Resilient Nation / 94

Chapter 6
Saving a Billion Lives / 117

Notes /138

Introduction

If there is one thing that history tells us unequivocally, it is that there is no area across the globe that can be termed disaster-proof. Calamities have a knack of striking when least expected, and unfortunately, institutional systems are often found lacking in capability.

This is more germane to countries categorized as developing or underdeveloped. Disasters, whether earthquakes, cyclones, floods, volcanoes, famines, industrial accidents or epidemics, have the capacity to wreak havoc paralleled only by conflicts.

Every decade, half-a-million people lose their lives due to calamities, and the economic cost of these disasters is commensurately humongous. Yet, adequate expertise continues to be a rarity, even among people in key positions.

Unfortunately, not everyone realizes the importance of the subject that affects human existence in a profound manner. This is quite relevant in the Indian context.

Approximately, 60 per cent of India's land area is susceptible to earthquakes. Over 12 per cent of its land is prone to floods, while of 75 per cent its coastline is prone to cyclones and tsunamis. Nearly 68 per cent of its arable land is at risk of drought.[1] In addition, there is also the risk of emergencies in the chemical, biological and nuclear domains.

It is remarkably perplexing how disaster management received inadequate attention for decades, even post independence. Arguably, the colonial hangover continued to afflict the political-administrative systems even after the imperial masters departed.

Also, in the hierarchy of national needs, other issues demanded more pressing attention. For instance, defence and food security. Yet, India was by no means a country not familiar with disasters. It faced, rather stoically, some of the biggest calamities the earth has ever seen.

The Bengal famine happened in 1943, when 3 million or 30 lakh people died of hunger—10 times the number of people who lost their lives during the atomic bombing of Hiroshima and Nagasaki put together. However, it hardly gets commensurate attention in academic or media discourses.

The Bengal famine was a manufactured disaster where strategic objectives of colonialists carried more weight than basic human values. Food, of which there arguably was no shortage, was diverted to armies fighting the world war, while hunger wiped out an entire population.

The tyranny of colonial rule ended after India gained independence in 1947, yet the discipline of disaster management did not get the attention it deserved.

In 1984, the Bhopal gas tragedy happened. In one of the worst industrial disasters, over 15,000 people perished, when tons of methyl isocyanate escaped an insecticide plant. Half-a-million others suffered serious respiratory or eye-related ailments. Many were rendered blind.

However, unfortunately, things did not change despite these huge tragedies. The nation witnessed many other disasters, small and big, in the next decades as well. The inability of the administrative mechanism to deal with emergency situations remained a constant.

In 2001, when India had just begun its Republic Day celebrations on 26 January, a massive earthquake measuring 6.9 on the Richter scale razed entire localities in the country's western-most district of Kutch in Gujarat. The estimated death toll was 13,805, and 167,000 were injured.[2]

The three episodes mentioned above—the Bengal famine, the Bhopal gas tragedy and the Kutch earthquake—belong to different eras.

The Bengal famine was the creation of an insensitive foreign power. The Bhopal gas tragedy demonstrates the helplessness of a fledgling nation that placed emergency response lower in the hierarchy among the plethora of its other pressing needs. The Kutch earthquake was a tragedy of unthinkable magnitude. Yet, it also marked a turning point for India in the field of disaster management. Narendra Modi, who became chief minister (CM) a few months after the quake, led Gujarat's efforts in mission mode as the region was rebuilt at a record pace.

The United Nations declared the 1990s as the 'International Decade for Natural Disaster Reduction' with the aim of cajoling nations to develop models of better disaster preparedness. For India, the turning point came after the Kutch earthquake.

Narendra Modi spearheaded Gujarat's reconstruction efforts, but it was not the first time that he worked in a disaster-hit zone. Not many know that in 1979, young Modi toiled in the watery swathes of Morbi town in Gujarat after it was ravaged by a deadly flood caused by one of the worst dam breaches in history. As a social worker and activist, he gained wide experience in handling diverse situations.

However, when Narendra Modi took over his first administrative job as the CM of Gujarat, there was much that was needed to be done in the domain of disaster risk reduction (DRR) in India. During his work as CM and post 2014 as prime minister (PM), the undeterred Modi played a pivotal role in shaping and augmenting India's capacity.

After the Kutch earthquake, CM Modi worked on his

Aapda me Avsar (opportunity in adversity) model and introduced the concept of increased community participation in disaster management.

The Gujarat State Disaster Management (GSDM) Act was introduced in 2003, which became a precursor to the Disaster Management Act, 2005. Gujarat developed institutions and frameworks for capacity building for disaster management and preparedness, especially with a focus on grassroots level.

Narendra Modi has continued this work as the PM of India. He took a number of steps to strengthen the DRR apparatus in the country.

An unprecedented challenge, that of the Covid-19 pandemic, had come into being. However, despite facing greater challenges, India handled this adversity better than even global superpowers. It was one of the few nations that could develop its own vaccines. It took care of its teeming masses of people. It also ensured that the economic engine of progress kept moving. Even the most die-hard of cynics were forced to acknowledge the extraordinary resolve and resilience shown by the nation. A democract in Narendra Modi managed all this with his time-tested approach of involving the people.

In the last two decades, India has begun moving towards a zone where it is more prepared and can respond systematically to emergencies. This book seeks to trace the important episodes in this ongoing journey related to the paradigm shift in India's disaster management mechanism and preparedness capacities.

While the changes India has undergone in the soon-to-be-completed 2014–24 decade in areas like social welfare, international affairs, infrastructure and economy are well known and documented, there are other equally important areas where substantial work has been accomplished. DRR is one such domain. In this book, an effort is made to understand

Narendra Modi's approach towards creating a resilient India. The book is a repository of knowledge on how he as the prime minister and in various other capacities before, sought to bring succour to the disaster-affected regions and their population. This volume, while eschewing any political polemic, seeks to provide a detailed account of those efforts, often through conversations with eyewitnesses and those on the ground.

This concise volume is also an attempt to provide practical real-life strategies in the ever-evolving domain of disaster management, sustainability and preparedness. For those interested in history, this book traces the journey of India from being an extremely vulnerable to becoming a much more prepared and resilient nation.

Additionally, it also is a compilation of lessons that Narendra Modi learnt and implemented during his work in Morbi, Kutch and Uttarakhand, as well as during Covid-19, and other contemporary crises that India has witnessed.

Having been among the most influential figures in global history, it is inevitable that aspects of his personal journey would find themselves intertwined with the march of the young nation of over a billion minds. Many of the lessons drawn are valuable in a diverse range of contexts. These lessons provide an idea of the country's journey through some of the most difficult times it has faced.

The first chapter of the book picks up an episode from history that reveals the challenges faced by India. It is about the Morbi dam breach and the role Narendra Modi and other volunteers played in helping a disaster struck region. The second chapter deals with an even more terrifying episode—the Kutch earthquake. The earthquake, however, was followed by the most efficient exercise in Indian history to rebuild a disaster struck region. The third chapter explores the pioneering initiatives Narendra Modi undertook as

Gujarat's CM to strengthen the state's capacity. The focus of the fourth chapter is on the significant measures India undertook post 2014 to become a more resilient nation. The fifth chapter examines India's effective response to the Covid-19 pandemic, a litmus test of the nation's ability to navigate through a significant calamity.

The anecdotes, quotes mentioned in the chapters, delineating the PM's experiences and contributions to the management and discourse of disaster management have been compiled from the personal interviews, interactions and meetings conducted by in-house teams.

Not only will these case studies and lessons make you more aware as a citizen or a professional, they also are an effective framework for taking adversity head-on and developing leadership potential.

Chapter 1

The Tears of Morbi 1979

A NATION UNPREPARED

On many occasions, the destruction or disasters that befall people are natural, and they inflict damage with surprise, like the terrible 100-feet tsunami that swept localities in Tamil Nadu and other states of India in December 2004.[1]

An earthquake of a massive 9.1 magnitude occurred off the coast of Sumatra in Indonesia, sending a series of waves that travelled across the Indian Ocean. Over 2,00,000 people lost their lives while millions of others were displaced.[2] The nation and the world watched nature's fury rather helplessly. The disaster was a grim pointer to how fragile human existence can be.

There are other instances, however, where tragedies happen as a result of human negligence or, perhaps, lack of capability or judgement. These can be termed man-made disasters but are no less lethal than the natural ones. Internal strife and external conflicts are capable of wreaking incalculable damage on people or a region. On other occasions, tragedies occur when systems simply not equipped to assess or deal with calamities.

The waves that swept away thousands of men, women and children in a sleepy Gujarati town—Morbi—on the banks of Machhu River in 1979 were not the product of a war or strife.

Nature's fury, undoubtedly, played its role. However, there has been a raging debate on if the destruction was purely an act of nature or a tragedy that occurred in the absence of an appropriate disaster response. India as an independent nation had just completed three decades. Years of subjugation and neglect had left a system that would often let the people down in times of dire need. Even if one was to consider it an act of God, as the authorities back in the day insisted, it occurred at a time when the administrative machinery was hardly prepared to deal with large-scale calamities.

That is what the serene and peaceful town of Morbi faced and endured three decades after the great famine in Bengal.

A TOWN SUBMERGED

Morbi or Morvi in Saurashtra region's Rajkot district is known for its prosperous ceramic trade. The majestic town grew on the banks of the Machhu River, which fertilizes the area. Independent India needed dams. They were hailed as the temples of a new nation. Following this necessity, a dam was constructed on the Machhu River in 1959 to irrigate the fields. A second dam known as Machhu II was built some years later in 1972. Machhu II had a catchment area of nearly 2,000 sq. km and was much bigger in capacity than Machhu I.[3]

All seemed normal till 11 August 1979, when the region was lashed with a particularly heavy rainfall. Often parched, Morbi and other areas of Gujarat normally long for rains. That fateful day, the people of the region had little idea of the unspeakable agony that the downpour and the resulting deluge were about to inflict.

In the town, people did not have even the slightest inkling that the dam built to irrigate the fields in the region would prove to be too frail to stop the rising waters. However, as a result of overtopping in the backdrop of incessant rain, a portion of the earthen embankment caved in.

Without much warning, and within minutes of the dam breach, wave after wave of destruction was unleashed on the adjoining areas, including the calm, unsuspecting town. The low-lying areas were among the first to be inundated.

The other parts of the town also did not fare better. By the afternoon, the entire population of Morbi had rushed out of their homes to save themselves. Those who could get out were fortunate. Estimates of the toll ranged from a couple of thousand to up to 20,000.[4] The economic cost ran into millions of rupees.

Words fail to describe the heart-rending scene at the once boisterous Morbi. The area was littered with corpses. Many bodies had become bloated and were in a terribly decomposed state.

Technological innovations, including means of communication that are available today, did not exist. On top of that, managing a disaster of the scale that hit Morbi would have been a challenge even for a more advanced and affluent country. Today, to address the disaster-related challenges, India has the world's single largest force dedicated to an efficient and effective disaster response. It is known by the name of National Disaster Response Force (NDRF).[5]

The state government under the Congress leader and then CM Babubhai Patel tried to support the people. Efforts were made to rush supplies to the thousands displaced. Cutting across party lines, all social and political organizations mobilized help.

Yet, it was a scenario for which the government was hardly prepared. A few days later, PM Indira Gandhi also visited the area. Naturally, when tall leaders visited the area, people gave vent to their anger.

Morbi needed immediate relief. It is in times of calamity that the obvious limitations of disaster handling came to the fore in the most grievously painful manner. The cataclysm highlighted the need for better disaster management systems and proactive measures.

THE FIRST RESPONDERS

The first few hours are crucial in the management of any catastrophic event. In the case of incidents like floods, timely warnings could allow people to move to safer places. A lot of destruction can be managed by quick mobilization of resources. Those who arrive at the scene and provide immediate relief are the first responders to any crisis. They play a significant role as they can save lives and attend to immediate and pressing relief needs. These first responders can be professionals like firefighters, volunteers or social organizations. In 2016, the National Disaster Management Authority (NDMA) introduced the Aapda Mitra scheme to prepare community volunteers with the necessary skills to address the community's requirements in a post-disaster scenario.[6]

In flood-hit Morbi, in addition to the government machinery, many social organizations, including the Rashtriya Swayamsewak Sangh (RSS), rushed to the aid of the people. Hundreds of volunteers, guided by senior leadership of the RSS, including Laxmanrao Inamdar (popularly known as Vakeel Saheb), Keshavrao Deshmukh, Pravinbhai Maniar, Keshubhai Patel, etc., hit the ground running and took the lead in carrying out the relief work.

Narendra Damodardas Modi, then 29, worked as a young *pracharak* of the RSS. On the day when the deluge devastated Morbi, he was in Kerala as part of his organizational duties. It was a time before the advent of the 24×7 information age. However, the moment he received the news, he decided to rush to Morbi. Having ascertained the magnitude of the tragedy in advance,

Narendra Modi also conveyed messages to his network of RSS volunteers, asking them to reach the beleaguered town.

During a speech delivered in Morbi in 2017, Prime Minister Narendra Modi gave an account of the events. 'On August 11, 1979, the Machhu dam disaster happened. That day, I was in Thiruvananthapuram in Kerala, and by the morning of the 13th, I was in Morbi. The RSS workers were on the streets, helping remove corpses and extending humanitarian assistance,' he said.[7]

Young Modi who was a *vibhag* (divisional) pracharak of the RSS and had proven his leadership abilities during the grim and dark days of the Emergency (1975–77) in the years prior to the Morbi floods. The senior leadership of the RSS was jailed during the Emergency, as were the top leaders of many political parties.

The leadership of the campaign against the undemocratic step taken by the Indira Gandhi regime had fallen on the shoulders of younger leaders like Narendra Modi. He had managed to evade arrest and carried out substantial work in creating awareness against the draconian step. His leadership skills were again sought in Morbi.

Having reached the flood-hit town, Narendra Modi spent the first few days contributing to the rescue and relief effort. Treatises on crisis and disaster management emphasize the importance of speedy and decisive action. Thus, it is unlikely that he would have delved into extensive volumes on the subject, and it is unlikely that any books could have guided the volunteers in dealing with the horrifying damage.

Narendra Modi and other volunteers who reached Morbi had to arrive on foot as roads and lanes were flooded. 'We had to walk for 1–2 km to reach Morbi. It was a terrible sight, with animal and human corpses hanging on electric wires. There was no electricity, no drinking water,' says RSS worker Girish Bhatt.

Guided by instinct, an intuitive Modi did what he later perfected as an administrator. Along with RSS volunteers, he assessed the situation and created a detailed plan through which teams were assigned specific tasks to address the different problems arising from the tragedy.

Governments can take time before they can choose a course of action. But for the young activist Modi, there was only one course of action, and that was to reach the people and find ways to alleviate their suffering.

'For over a month, I spent time in Morbi during the saddest moments, removing mud, carrying dead animals, and performing funeral rites for families who had lost their loved ones,' PM Modi recounted during his speech in Morbi in 2017.

A *Times of India* report dated 30 September 1979, says that under the leadership of Narendra Modi, the RSS formed the P¯ur Pidit Sahayata Samiti (Flood Victims Relief Committee). The report mentions that the committee raised ₹14 lakh for building homes for the victims. It provided free medical aid and distributed food grains and clothes for those affected by the disaster. In addition, it also mentions a cheque of ₹5 lakh from the RSS's Maharashtra wing handed over to Narendra Modi for relief work in the affected areas around Morbi.[8]

Morbi needed all the help it could muster, and the role that RSS volunteers and other social organizations performed was crucial. In their well-researched book *No One Had a Tongue to Speak: The Untold Story of One of History's Deadliest Floods*, Utpal Sandesara and Tom Wooten mention the major role played by the RSS and other organizations. As they write in the book, 'By all accounts, the Home Guards and members of voluntary organisations—above all the Hindu nationalist Rashtriya Swayamsewak Sangh (RSS)—undertook the bulk of the most difficult removal. Donning gloves and facemasks, they threw themselves into the macabre task with grim determination.'[9]

The authors in their detailed account mention that the Rajkot collectorate had contacted a number of organizations, and the RSS, Ramakrishna Ashram and members of the Swaminarayan sect were among those who responded with alacrity.

They pointed out that the relief work was also taking a psychological toll on the volunteers as many of them had never ever touched a dead body before. The RSS called its workers from different districts of Gujarat to assist with the relief efforts. They were assigned tasks based on their availability and were accommodated in camps established on the outskirts of Morbi.

Apart from Sandesara and Wooten's book, the work done by Narendra Modi and RSS volunteers is also etched in the memories of the victims who were beneficiaries of the relief efforts. 'Our village was heavily waterlogged due to the flood and food and other essentials became scarce. At that time, Narendra Modi came to our village with other RSS workers and distributed essential items to hundreds of people,' recollects Habib Devakadiya, a survivor of the Morbi dam breach.

Devakadiya recalls that the volunteers worked tirelessly and yet showed no sign of fatigue. 'We kept working relentlessly for 50 days at a stretch. One could find people looking for their lost loved ones in the alleyways that were laced with mud and sludge. This went on for the first 15–20 days,' says Dalpatbhai Rathva, one of the volunteers.

Leaving every other pursuit aside, an empathetic Modi had stayed in the flood-hit town for nearly six weeks. The volunteers would work for hours at a stretch. The local population could sense the motivation with which the Sangh volunteers went about their work. The recognition in turn lent a sense of pride in the volunteers and doubled their motivation level.

However, Narendra Modi could sense the prevailing sense of hopelessness among the residents of Morbi. He understood that the key to overcoming this challenge lay in people themselves coping with the situation and taking the lead in their own rehabilitation. With this in mind, he wrote a motivational letter addressed primarily to the youth of Morbi. He tried to ensure that a copy of this letter reached every household. His message not only kindled a spirit of self-reliance among the youth but also guaranteed that they discovered significant roles in the revitalization of their beloved city.

KEY TAKEAWAY

The role of first responders in a disaster is extremely significant. For nations to be prepared for disasters, there should be a strategy for the creation of dedicated first responders. India now has a dedicated force in the NDRF, in addition to personnel of fire services, police, and volunteers from schemes like Aapda Mitra, etc., who can be the first responders. However, it must be kept in mind that first responders need to be highly motivated and well-trained. First responders need to be self-starters who do not wait for someone to point out their duties. They should be able to assess a situation and chart out a course of action.

COORDINATION AND SYSTEMATIC APPROACH

Disaster management and mitigation efforts often fail to meet the desired objectives due to a lack of systematic approach on the ground. Mobilizing and managing resources is one of the major initial challenges for any relief effort. Preparing a systematic plan of response can help immensely in ensuring a speedy recovery. The best-laid plans on paper are meaningless if they are not implemented with the same efficiency. This is as true of disaster relief scenarios as of any other human pursuit.

At the time of the Morbi dam breach, India was yet to develop an effective disaster management and preparedness mechanism. Gujarat, which is today a pioneer in DRR, was not prepared to handle the calamity in 1979. Volunteers played a crucial role in handling such a situation, but the lack of a coordinated and systematic approach was still palpable.

The receding waters had left behind a devastating trail of destruction. Narendra Modi began coordinating with the teams of volunteers who arrived from different districts of Gujarat to contribute to the rehabilitation operations. Teams of volunteers were deployed to clean roads, clear muck from the houses, and pull out the bodies and cremate them.

He, along with the volunteers, also arranged food for the survivors. The Morbi tragedy was a life-changing event for many who were involved in the rescue and relief operations. RSS workers like Bhikhubhai Pambhar from Junagadh, who picked up decaying bodies and cremated them, testify that they were inspired by the dedication and endurance of Narendra Modi and his group of volunteers. Pambhar remembers that the hardworking Modi would carry sacks of grain on his back. He worked tirelessly and that gained him the respect of other volunteers.

Another volunteer, Sanjay Shah, recounts that the conditions in Morbi at that time were terrifying, to say the least. The sight haunts him to this day. There were corpses in every part of the town. The scenes unnerved him. However, senior volunteers like Narendra Modi motivated and encouraged everyone. 'He (Narendra Modi) was already involved in the process of cremation. He took the lead in doing all the work in accordance with the plans drawn up by the RSS team,' says Shah.

A particularly difficult task was to retrieve the bodies, as many of them were in a swollen or sometimes disfigured state. And it was not just human bodies. Corpses of animals were strewn across the area.

They had to be buried as the stench had become unbearable. There was also the fear that putrefying corpses could turn into sources of infection and disease. The stench after a flood is practically unbearable. The photo of then PM Indira Gandhi covering her nose with a handkerchief made it to the front covers of some publications, some locals remember.

Even the local authorities, including police, struggled to tackle this challenge. Disposing the putrid corpses was one of the most difficult tasks that Narendra Modi and his fellow volunteers decided to take up. RSS leaders tried to keep the morale high so that the volunteers could carry on. Yet, disposing of bloated bodies was not easy. It was a kind of work that even the authorities shied away from. Young Modi and other volunteers, however, decided that someone had to do it.

Pambhar provides an eye-witness account. 'There was an old age home in Morbi where 23 out of the 30 residents died. When the volunteers visited the area, it was full of sludge. We had to put masks on our faces to avoid the stench,' says Pambhar. He had to lift a decaying body.

'I gathered courage and took hold of the hand, trying to lift it. However, it slipped away,' he recalls. Narendra Modi sensed Pambhar's nervousness. He asked Pambhar to steel himself. 'Narendra Modi reminded me of the importance of our work. After that, I gathered courage and we took all the 23 decaying bodies out and cremated them,' Pambhar recounts.

Relentless Modi kept moving from one part of the town to another, gauging what effort was needed and where. In one of the areas, a body was stuck in the sludge in a particularly unyielding way.

As the others struggled to find a way, Narendra Modi

managed to pull it off. He suggested that bodies could be wrapped in cloth so that they were not dismembered while being pulled up or lifted. This was a useful, practical advice.

Pradip Vala, a resident of Morbi, was associated with the BJP's youth wing, Akhil Bharatiya Vidyarthi Parishad (ABVP) at that time. He was part of a team that assigned the responsibility of carrying rescue and relief work in an engineering college, located in Morbi. They found human and animal corpses as far up as the sixth floor of the hostel building.

However, the obstacles they faced while carrying out the rescue and relief work at a temple were even higher. The temple, located at a slightly higher altitude than the surrounding areas, had offered shelter to the people during previous floods. The deluge of 1979, however, was of a different magnitude.

The temple premises were flooded, and atleast 100 innocent lives seeking shelter there, were lost.[10] 'Only a young priest, who managed to climb the temple top, survived. Rescuing him required both skill and courage. The temple was still inundated. Narendra Modi and the other *karyakartas* (workers) saved him,' adds Vala.

The state of the Shantivan Ashram in Morbi was unbelievably appalling. The Ashram was set up by a saint called Keshvananda Bapu from Girnar. Narendra Modi, during his visits to Morbi, would make it a point to visit the Ashram to meet Keshavananda Bapu.

'This ashram was also devastated in the deluge and around 12 people were found dead on its premises. Since the bodies remained undiscovered for four days, a horrible stench filled up the air. Most people were reluctant to go inside. Narendra Modi, however, came forward and carried the bodies out and arranged their cremation,' says Janakbhai Kotak, former mayor of Rajkot who accompanied him to Morbi.

The volunteers arranged oil, diesel, petrol and wood for the cremation. Arranging dry wood was not easy as the entire state of Gujarat had received heavy rains. In some instances, even the deceased person's family members were uncomfortable cremating their dead relatives. The Sangh volunteers stepped forward and a collective cremation was conducted at the local cremation ground.

As mentioned earlier, relief work during a disaster is not like normal work. Unexpected hitches delay the progress; therefore, workers have to be resourceful and think outside the box to come up with solutions.

'There was an instance when the wood for cremation would not burn, as it was quite damp. We took out diesel from the tank of a vehicle belonging to a police officer and poured it over the wood to light the pyre,' recalls Pambhar.

Though extremely difficult, the task of cremating hundreds of bloated corpses was just one of the many problems that Morbi faced. It was a town grappling with a deluge of challenges. The state government machinery and central agencies were doing all they could. Yet, they needed support from other organizations that played a key role in relief efforts.

There were numerous challenges that Morbi faced following the dam breach such as the displacement of thousands, including women, children; the need for immediate medical attention to the injured; the entire town was covered in sludge, sanitation was to be ensured; those rendered homeless needed to be fed; health concerns were to be addressed such as the threat of the spread of an epidemic; destructed infrastructure such as power supply, roads were to be repaired and made functional again; livelihood of the people and economic support to the economically weaker section was to be restored, amongst others.

The RSS volunteers worked in tandem with the local authorities and groups to address each challenge. Even at that time, young Modi's approach was quite methodical. Many RSS volunteers recall that it was his systematic approach that added speed to the relief work.

Hashu Pandya, an RSS volunteer, was a student at that time. 'Narendra Modi divided the relief work into various activities and assigned them to people systematically. Different tasks like cleaning, food preparation, food distribution, transporting affected people to Rajkot hospital and so on were assigned to different groups of volunteers,' he recalls.

Kishor Lakde of Vadodara took leave from his job in the railways to rush to Morbi with his friends. Narendra Modi, who was overseeing the relief operations, assigned them the task of cleaning houses that were filled with mud and sludge. The cleaning teams consisted of around five people per team. They were armed with spades and instructed on how to clear the filth. 'At the end of each day, a highly organized Modi would hold meetings to take stock of our progress. The team was given a week to complete the task. Within that time frame, they managed to clean an entire colony,' recounts Lakde.

Locals recall how Narendra Modi undertook the cleaning and restoration work for a mosque in Morbi. Eid was approaching, and he wanted the mosque to be in a restored state so that people could offer their prayers on the day of the festival. The volunteers, again, worked with zeal, and the task was accomplished.

As some were cleaning the muck and others disposing of corpses, another set of volunteers was working to restore amenities and distribute food grains among the survivors. Volunteers like Pradip Vala provide testimony that Narendra Modi was especially particular about the systematic distribution of the food grains. 'Often, he would carry sacks of grain on his own back to deliver them to the needy,' says Vala. He was keen to ensure that no needy person was left unattended.

'A Congress worker lived near a temple. His house was filled with sludge. There were 2–3 bodies at his place as well,' says Vala. There used to be bitter political rivalry between the Sangh and Congress workers. However, the moment the Sangh volunteers arrived, the Congressman could not control his emotions. 'What took you so long? My house is in such a terrible condition. Tell me what am I supposed to do? Although this is the government's responsibility, please help me now,' the Congress worker shouted. A compassionate Modi assured the person that they had come to help him. He asked him to sit on the side while the Sangh volunteers got his place cleaned, recalls Vala.

'Narendra *bhai* used to plan everything. He asked us to survey houses and make a plan for distribution of food based on the requirements. No house was allowed to be left out. He even told us to respect the dignity of the people receiving aid. He would tell them, "We are only giving you what is rightfully yours, this is not a favour",' recalls Nagarbhai Chavda, one of the volunteers from Rajkot.

Many people would come to meet Narendra Modi, offering donations such as small amounts of money, blankets or grains. The karyakartas would then distribute these donations to those in need.

A makeshift kitchen was set up by the RSS karyakartas to provide food to the surviving flood victims. Food was prepared and packed in packets. Different teams would then take the food to people in different localities.

Disaster scenarios can be extremely harsh on infants, pregnant women, differently abled people and the elderly. In any relief and rescue effort, as far as possible, it is important to factor in the specific needs of the affected and vulnerable population.

Even though calamities hardly spare any section, it is also a reality that the poor often suffer the hardest blow. While other sections may be able to garner resources for recover, the poorest or those pushed into poverty by the disaster face a much steeper climb. Naturally, the Sangh volunteers focussed their maximum energy in providing succour to the vulnerable.

KEY TAKEAWAY

Disasters bring with them a myriad of problems one after the other. The relief workers and other stakeholders contributing to disaster management need to have a systematic approach to prioritize each of the activities and ensure justified allocation of necessary resources and support mechanisms. It is quite important that the infants, women, the elderly, differently abled people and the economically weaker sections are given priority.

COMPREHENSIVE RESPONSE

Disaster scenarios are ones involving complex challenges that require comprehensive and holistic solutions. During disasters, relief workers need to think on their feet and respond to developing situations accordingly. Leadership during disasters is about the ability to draw a road map to bring lives back to normal.

Morbi was the first experience for Narendra Modi in leading a disaster-handling exercise. No doubt, it was a testing time. However, it also gave ample opportunity for his instincts to get sharpened and insights to acquire depth. This experience would later prove invaluable when he turned administrator in the aftermath of an even greater disaster—the Kutch earthquake in 2001.

The lessons learned in the aftermath of the Morbi disaster were with CM Modi when he started the Kutch relief and rehabilitation effort. In Morbi, he had led teams to rescue, retrieve dead bodies and cremate, sanitize the area, distribute relief materials, etc. He spent the initial months in Kutch as a volunteer performing tasks similar to those he undertook in Morbi.

Those who have worked with Narendra Modi often speak about the great attention that he paid to detail and the stress he laid on meticulous planning. As he led the relief efforts, these attributes proved to be of good use.

A key concern in any disaster situation is that one problem can lead to another. Since the conditions are often not sanitary, there is a constant threat of an epidemic outbreak. Even in contemporary history, there have been instances where an epidemic outbreak has compounded the misery inflicted on a disaster struck region.

For instance, after the massive earthquake in Haiti in 2010 when 2,00,000 people lost their lives, a cholera outbreak infected 8,20,000 people. Of these, 10,000 are estimated to have died due to the disease.[11]

In the case of Morbi, the Sangh leadership made arrangements for volunteers who rushed to Morbi from Rajkot. They were administered vaccines to prevent them from catching cholera. Furthermore, the volunteers also made arrangements for doctors so that they could be brought to the town to aid its ailing population. They began a vaccination drive as well. 'In addition to the clean-up, a vaccination drive was organized. Camps were set up in different areas to administer vaccines and prevent the spread of diseases. Narendra Modi reached out to the government at that time and informed them about the vaccination plans, seeking assistance in providing vaccines for the drive to safeguard the people,' recalls Damodarbhai Patel, another volunteer.

Teams of doctors came from different parts of Gujarat at the call of Narendra Modi and other Sangh seniors. A temporary dispensary was also set up there, as the government hospital was in a dismal condition. Medicines were also sent from Rajkot. A mobile team of 20–30 doctors was designated to go around in the nearby villages. 'The volunteers and state government worked in unison to ensure that medical aid reached people,' says Girish Bhatt.

Apart from the doctors, the Sangh workers were also making efforts to get all kinds of skilled personnel that could put life in Morbi back on track. On the first day of the rescue efforts, insightful Modi tasked his team to clean the market space of its sludge. Fresh commodities, whenever they arrive, needed a clean place to be stored.

Volunteers also cleaned the houses of mud and sludge and made them inhabitable. But many houses were destroyed. Those fully destroyed were to be rebuilt and those partially damaged were to be repaired. The Sangh leadership decided to build houses for those who lost theirs completely. Narendra Modi also took the lead in bringing skilled workers to repair houses.

'During the Morbi tragedy, my father received a phone call from Narendra Modi, who expressed a need for skilled workers such as technicians, electricians and plumbers. He requested that my father assemble a team of these skilled workers and send them to Morbi, where their expertise was greatly needed,' says Narendra Sonagra from Vadodara.

Many RSS workers received similar calls from him. As a result, a large group of skilled workers reached Morbi to make the town habitable again.

According to locals, a large number of houses were constructed with the help of the RSS workers at the time. There were no construction workers available. However, Narendra Modi managed to contact someone and workers came from Andhra Pradesh, recalls Dr Jayanti Bhadesia from Morbi who witnessed his efforts during the floods. Girish Bhatt provides a detailed first-hand account. 'After cleanliness, we started the rehabilitation process. Many *kutcha* houses had been destroyed. Similarly, many *pucca* houses were extensively damaged. A plan was made for rehabilitation and RSS volunteers got involved in the process,' he says.

Bhatt adds that the trust, Pūr Pidit Sahayata Samiti, played a crucial role in the rehabilitation work. 'About 400 houses were reconstructed, with approximately 200 of them in Morbi and 200 in two villages in Wankaner and Maliya *tehsils* surrounding Morbi. Narendra Modi, in this rehabilitation plan, got in touch with Subhash Mehta, who was an old acquaintance of his from Ahmedabad but then moved to the US. Mehta came back after learning of the damage caused in the floods. He was a civil engineer. Under the rehabilitation work, pucca homes were designed with two rooms, a kitchen and a store,' says Bhatt.

Mehta vividly remembers the task he and his team accomplished after he arrived from the US. 'I was in Morbi for two years as project engineer, under the guidance of Narendra Modi and other senior leaders of Sangh. We made a list of the people whose houses were completely destroyed and built new ones. Villages like Nagdavas were decimated. Narendra Modi arranged for me to have a jeep whenever I needed to travel. My team came down to Morbi to work on the reconstruction. We gathered funds from all over the world and used them to build houses,' he says.

'RSS chief Balasaheb Deoras visited Morbi and dedicated the houses to the people. When I returned to New York, Narendra Modi wrote me a letter of appreciation. He wrote that the people were extremely happy, just like they are at the birth of a child,' recalls Mehta.

As Morbi painfully trudged towards a semblance of normalcy, one of the tasks that continued to be unaccomplished was the restoration of electricity. Officials of the power department were willing to restore it but they faced a problem. The gushing flood waters had uprooted scores of electric poles. Adequate manpower to raise them again was not available. The Sangh volunteers and others again chipped in. They took on the responsibility of erecting poles and assisted technicians from the electricity department in ensuring a steady supply of electricity.

When Narendra Modi led the relief activity in Morbi, it was not just immediate relief that was on his mind. He had a vision of ensuring comprehensive rehabilitation. His philosophy of 'Aapda me Avsar' and 'Build Back Better' that he proved successfully during the Kutch earthquake of 2001, first began taking shape during the Morbi relief effort.

During their interaction with the local people, the volunteers would often encounter those who rued the destruction Morbi had faced. The devastation has taken the town 25 years back, they would lament. Narendra Modi would assure them that Morbi would bounce back and their businesses would flourish once again.

For centuries, Morbi held a distinguished reputation as a hub for the manufacturing of 'naliya', clay roof tiles traditionally employed for roofing and the creation of mosaic tiles. This industry was completely destroyed. During rehabilitation efforts, people were given the confidence that they could resume this business. This tile production was encouraged on a priority basis.

In the initial days, Narendra Modi's attention was focused on relief. However, as days passed, he began to look deeper into the aspects related to rehabilitation—how to convert the disaster into an opportunity to offer a better life to the people of Morbi.

In the aftermath of the Morbi dam accident, a great debate brewed as to how such a calamity could have taken place. There were cries to determine accountability. There were also political battles over the tragedy. According to some records, it even got registered in the early editions of the Guinness Book of World Records as the 'worst dam burst'.[12]

Sandesara and Wooten's book provides a detailed account of the shortcomings and how the administrative set up dealt with the efforts to investigate the disaster. But what became clear from the Morbi dam breach and other calamities was that despite decades of independence, India was yet to develop a sturdier disaster management apparatus.

However, it would still take decades before India would develop a more comprehensive legal-administrative mechanism.

KEY TAKEAWAY

Disaster management has to be a comprehensive exercise not limited to relief and rescue. It should cover all aspects of bringing community life back to normal, from rehabilitation to restoring livelihoods. Though hard to imagine, disasters can also be converted into opportunities to deliver a better life to the victims. The Disaster Management Act that came into force in 2005 looks at many of these aspects.

PREPARING FOR THE FUTURE

In Morbi, Narendra Modi got a first-hand experience of carrying out rescue and relief work. Morbi benefitted due to the presence of him and his team in its hour of crisis. However, it also gave ground-level insights to him. As a policymaker in the later years, this first-hand knowledge played a great role in shaping his decisions.

As CM of Gujarat and as PM of India, Narendra Modi has stressed on a 5R framework in the area. These five Rs were: Rescue, Relief, Restoration, Rehabilitation and Rebuilding. It was in Morbi that Narendra Modi first worked in these areas.

The horrible tragedy in Morbi left a deep imprint on his mind. He became aware of the deep gaps in the state and country's preparedness in dealing with events of a calamitous nature. He also witnessed how there were no effective provisions to ensure suitable maintenance of massive infrastructures like dams. In 2021, with Narendra Modi as the PM, Parliament brought in an effective law to ensure safety of dams.

Government data reveals that India ranks as the third-largest nation in terms of dam ownership, following China and the USA. India has over 6,000 large dams, with roughly 80 per cent of them surpassing 25 years in age. Astonishingly, nearly 234 dams in the country are over a century old and remain operational.[13] 'The Dam Safety Bill provides for adequate surveillance, inspection, operation, and maintenance of all the large dams in the country so as to prevent dam failure-related disasters,' the Modi government said in a statement issued after the passage of the bill in Parliament.[14] The measures that Narendra Modi took to ensure a more resilient India, form the subject matter of the succeeding chapters.

In Morbi, Narendra Modi not only witnessed the horrific ground realities of a disaster but actively led efforts for nearly two months to alleviate the suffering of the victims. From Morbi, the comprehensive idea of sustainable development of a resilient nation took root in his mind.

Chapter 2

Devastation in Kutch

A CATASTROPHE UNPRECEDENTED

Chobari, a tiny village in the heart of Kutch district, is a place that only a few people, even in Gujarat, had heard of. However, that changed in a matter of a single day.

On 26 January 2001, when India had just begun to celebrate its Republic Day, a massive intraplate earthquake, measuring 6.9 on the Richter scale, jolted Kutch.[1] The deadliest earthquake in contemporary Indian history had its epicentre a few kilometres southwest of the village of Chobari.

The effect of the earthquake was such that the ground continued to shake for nearly two minutes. Lakhs of people lost everything. Buildings built to provide shelter came crashing down. The estimated death toll was 13,805. The number of injured touched nearly 1,67,000, according to government estimates. Over 2 lakh houses collapsed, and over 9 lakh suffered damages.[2]

The Kutch earthquake was the worst recorded in India ever since the 1737 Calcutta earthquake, in which 300,000 people are estimated to have been killed. The 2001 earthquake was the worst natural disaster India had seen in half a century. It occurred quite close to the one Kutch had faced in June 1819. It affected 21 out of 25 districts of Gujarat, including Ahmedabad, Patan, Jamnagar, Rajkot and Surendranagar. The number of villages affected majorly by the disaster stood at 7,633[3]. The desert district of Kutch bore 90 per cent of the devastation caused by the earthquake.[4]

The earthquake was also followed by over 500 aftershocks, many of them of magnitude 3.0 and above. In Ahmedabad, 250 km east of the epicentre, around 80 high-rise buildings collapsed.[5]

Sprawling Kutch is not just the western-most part of India but also Gujarat's largest district. It is known across the world for its industrious and business-savvy people. Yet, on that fateful day, the region found itself broken and paralysed.

Utility infrastructure, including electricity, water supply, telecommunications, etc., was thoroughly disrupted. Public buildings like hospitals and schools were badly damaged.

Rescue efforts by both the central and state governments began immediately. Help and volunteers began to pour in from all sides. Many global organizations and countries were prompt in providing relief support. However, the scale of the calamity that came without warning was too large. Many social and voluntary organizations, including the RSS, made efforts to rescue the calamity-struck people.

Narendra Modi had been among the first responders to the Morbi dam breach in 1979. Twenty years later, he was again among the hundreds who rushed to Kutch.

'The day after the earthquake struck, he arrived in Kutch and spent his first night at a school located in Samakhiali, a town in Kutch district,' says Haresh Mulchandani, a former chief of the BJP unit in Bhachau, one of the four worst-affected towns in the district. The other three towns were Bhuj, Anjar and Rapar.

At that time, Narendra Modi was working as national general secretary of the BJP and stationed in New Delhi. However, learning of this disaster of an unprecedented magnitude in his home state, tender-hearted Modi immediately wanted to be with the people in their time of distress. Senior BJP and RSS leaders also asked him to reach the location and lead the disaster relief work.

In Kutch, Narendra Modi traversed village after village on foot as well as on a motorcycle. There were many in the region whom he knew intimately. He tried to reach out to all of them. However, simultaneously, he also began forming a strategy for relief work. He tried to make an assessment of the level of destruction in different areas and began preparing a plan for the initial relief and subsequent rehabilitation.

During his stay in Morbi after the dam breach, Narendra Modi had rescued people, pulled out dead bodies, arranged relief, managed resources, created plans for rehabilitation, etc. The Kutch earthquake was a disaster of a much larger magnitude. However, many of the challenges were common, and he had solutions that he learned from his previous experience. He put all he knew into practice.

The Kutch earthquake also led to a tectonic shift in Gujarat politics. The central leadership of the BJP chose Narendra Modi to become the CM of Gujarat a few months after the earthquake. As Gujarat's CM, Narendra Modi took a role in which he got the opportunity to contribute not only in rebuilding Kutch but also to develop an overall paradigm for disaster management. In fact, during that period, the world was already discussing and trying to create better models of disaster management that could help in reducing losses, both human and financial.

The United Nations (UN) had designated the 1990s as the 'International Decade of Natural Disaster Reduction.' The discussions and debate had continued into the next decade as well. In India, however, even after 50 years of independence, disaster mitigation and preparedness was unfortunately a rather neglected subject.

There was no detailed doctrine on preparedness. In 1999, just two years before Kutch earthquake, another disaster in the form of a super cyclone claimed around 10,000 lives in the eastern state of Odisha.[6] It had again exposed India's lack of preparedness when it came to calamitous situations. Subsequently, the Odisha cyclone led to the creation of a state disaster management body in the eastern state.[7]

However, it is the Kutch earthquake that thoroughly underlined the urgent need for India to prepare its own models for better disaster management and resilience. Most accounts hold the Kutch earthquake to be a turning point in India's journey towards greater DRR.

One of the significant impacts of the tragedy was that the domain of disaster management was shifted to the Union Home Ministry from the Union Agriculture Ministry, which was hardly equipped to deal with challenges in a rapidly urbanizing society. An even greater change was the disaster management law that Gujarat passed, followed by a similar legislation at the national level.

The NDRF was formed only after the Disaster Management Act was passed in 2005. The way Gujarat handled its toughest disaster and the lessons it drew from it left a deep imprint on the subsequent legislations.

Kutch was a moment that helped Modi in developing a model that can be useful for years to come, then it was a turning point in preparing better to handle tough situations in the future for the nation.

Before becoming Gujarat's CM, the few months spent at the ground level in Kutch, gave Narendra Modi deeper insights into what needed to be done. In Morbi, he had expressed his optimism that the city would again attain its prosperous nature. In Kutch, as Gujarat's CM, he actually worked to create Aapda me Avsar.

RESOURCEFULNESS: HARNESSING SOCIAL GOODWILL

It has been mentioned that Narendra Modi was one of the first persons to rush to Kutch in its hour of need. As a relief worker, the first two important things he did in Kutch were mobilizing people and begin procuring relief material.

He held meetings in Ahmedabad and Gandhinagar with party and Sangh workers from different parts of Gujarat, seeking to chalk out the next course of action. He met various organizations which could send people to Kutch. He contacted NGOs, industry houses and individuals who had the capacity to contribute substantial relief material.

As an RSS pracharak since the early 1970s, Gujarat BJP's organizational secretary and then national leader based in New Delhi, he had developed tremendous goodwill, and he was willing to reach out to organizations and well-meaning individuals who he believed would be of help for social good. Kutch was one such instance when he mobilized help from all he knew and more.

Despite the efforts of the government and the arrival of volunteers and social organizations, the resources were meagre. There were thousands of victims in relief camps or displaced here and there. Basic needs like food, water, clothing, blankets, etc., were not available in the required quantities.

Dilipbhai Deshmukh, an RSS worker, narrates how Narendra Modi utilized his goodwill towards generating resources for relief work in Kutch: 'Narendra Modi called the owner of Britannia Industries Nusli Wadia with a request about the supply of biscuits for the affected area. Wadia asked how many biscuits were needed. He responded that atleast 10 lakh cartons were needed for the people. In a remarkable display of generosity, Wadia donated an entire godown of biscuits,' says Deshmukh.

During his stay in Morbi, Narendra Modi had learned that

biscuits were useful as they could be stored and distributed easily. In Kutch, as a result of his effort and Wadia's magnanimity, thousands did not have to sleep on empty stomachs. Locals of Kutch remember how they survived on biscuit packets for days to this day. He also coordinated efforts to ensure that NGOs could provide meals twice a day to needy people.

By its very nature, a calamity puts the existing systems out of gear. New sources of food, shelter, manpower and other amenities become the need of the hour. In such circumstances, societal goodwill and the better nature of humanity have the power to elicit meaningful contributions.

Organizations including the RSS, BAPS (BAPS Swaminarayan Sanstha), Amritanandamayi Math, Jain Samaj, CII (Confederation of Indian Industry), FICCI (Federation of Indian Chambers of Commerce and Industry), Reliance Foundation, Tata group, L&T (Larsen & Toubro), Rotary Club, etc., were actively involved in the relief and rehabilitation. A collective of NGOs called Kutch Navnirman Abhiyan also played a significant role. Additionally, representatives of global organizations like World Bank, Asian Development Bank (ADB), United Nations Development Programme (UNDP), Red Cross, etc., were stationed in Kutch for months.

Kutch also received substantial help from the sizeable Gujarati diaspora spread across the world. Narendra Modi focussed on the idea of utilizing corporate social responsibility funds for relief and rehabilitation work.

In Anjar, former deputy mayor Bharat Shah recalls that Narendra Modi arranged trucks of packaged mineral water. Drinking water was a major concern. 'Some NGOs he contacted helped in the distribution of food, others helped in providing clothes. He asked smaller NGOs to adopt villages and bigger ones to help redevelop cities,' adds Shah.

Foresighted Modi believed that the government alone cannot do all that the devastated Kutch region required. He firmly emphasized that NGOs, the RSS, community and spiritual organizations had to take up a major role to supplement government efforts. He also maintained a list of NGOs while he was the BJP general secretary. He got in touch with the NGOs and worked in unison with them, helping in revival of the villages. Villages such as Bhimasar in Anjar, Manaba in Rapar, and several others were adopted by NGOs and re-developed, making them as models of reconstruction.

Haryana's CM Manohar Lal Khattar recalls that Narendra Modi reached out to the Haryana BJP workers and many resourceful people from the state.[8] Narendra Modi had been in charge of Haryana BJP since 1996. Many party workers reached Kutch on his call and offered their services.

The earthquake had struck in January, one of the coldest months in India. People were suffering due to the unbearable weather conditions. Apart from shelter, they needed warm clothing as well. Kind-hearted Modi, along with his team, tried to bring relief on this front. At that time, 1 lakh blankets were arranged from Jalandhar and other areas. Other essentials were also arranged.

Not only did he demonstrate resourcefulness, he also came up with innovative survival skills. There was a discussion between him and Radhanpur Member of Legislative Assembly (MLA) Shankar Chaudhary on whether they should procure pouches instead of water bottles.

'Narendra Modi favoured bottles reasoning that people could refill them for repeat use. They could also fill them with hot water and place them on their chests to stay warm. The weather was chilly. Surprisingly, many people actually followed this practice,' recalls Chaudhary.

Narendra Modi stayed with the workers in Kutch wherever possible—be it a partly destroyed school building or cattle shed. He led the team in taking out bodies and arranging proper cremation, like he had done two decades back in Morbi.

Those still stuck underneath the rubble had to be brought out. As compared to Morbi in 1979, the devastation in Kutch was at a much larger scale. Morbi had been a tough experience, but it had taught Modi many things. In Kutch, Narendra Modi led his team of workers with confidence and ensured they remained focussed.

Bharat Shah remembers the instance when news of a young boy trapped beneath the rubble reached Narendra Modi. He took swift action, contacting international rescue experts who successfully extricated the boy. Initial treatment was provided, although one leg had to be amputated. Following this, he was transferred to a navy hospital and later to a hospital in Pune, ultimately saving his life. 'The boy's parents had died in the earthquake but he was saved due to Narendra Modi's effort,' says Shah.

There are several examples of Narendra Modi's resourcefulness and timely intervention. His concerns, however, went beyond those of the other volunteers and even administrators. For instance, he wanted to protect the cattle that may have been trapped in the debris. He knew that domestic animals are important sources of livelihood for people and can financially sustain families who bore huge losses in the disaster. He also knew that the death of animals can lead to outbreak of diseases.

As was witnessed in Morbi, the disposal of animal carcasses becomes an onerous task. Indian cultural values also consider life divine in all its forms. So, while his team arranged biscuits and other food items, Narendra Modi made arrangements for the welfare of the cattle.

'He asked me to arrange fodder for them no matter what it

took. After two hours, he enquired again whether I had been able to arrange the feed. He expressed immense relief when I told him that it had been done,' recollects a BJP worker named Girish Dani.

Anil Pandya from Anjar says the presence of Narendra Modi also helped in bridging gaps between the society and the administration. 'He personally took stock of everything in Anjar such as medicine supply, number of deaths and number of injured people. Then he went to Gandhinagar and informed the officials about the situation and sought their help,' Anil states. Even though Narendra Modi was not a part of central government then, he was an important leader of the party and well-respected by all.

Along with leading relief and rehabilitation efforts, the idea of rebuilding Kutch was already taking shape in his mind. Nitin Bhardwaj, a Rajkot resident recalls the exact words the former had spoken, giving the people and volunteers a glimpse of his vision: *Aawo aafatne avsarma palatiye* (Let's convert disaster into an opportunity).

This concept brought energy and purpose in the minds of the volunteers, says Bharadwaj. Narendra Modi and the volunteers worked tirelessly towards the relief and rehabilitation of the survivors. However, he also kept his sights set towards building a better future for the people of Kutch.

Soon after, Narendra Modi became the CM of Gujarat, he gave his vision of Aapda me Avsar a shape.

KEY TAKEAWAY

For any disaster management exercise, stakeholders look up to strong and visionary leaders to give a roadmap. Any leader steering the work in a challenging environment earns respect and gains confidence of his team members by being hands-on. Those aware of ground realities can more readily come up with solutions, and the key to providing solutions often lies in resourcefulness.

LEADING FROM THE FRONT

The Kutch earthquake also led to tremors in Gujarat politics. The state was set for elections a year later, in 2002. The BJP government under PM Atal Bihari Vajpayee was in power at the centre. The ruling BJP leaders in Delhi wanted to ensure efficient rehabilitation. If Kutch had to be rebuilt, there was no person better than Narendra Modi.

Senior leaders were aware of his work. It was known to everyone in the party and the Sangh how he had worked in Morbi for months without a break. Volunteers who came back from Kutch recounted the passion that they witnessed in an impassioned Modi during the earthquake relief work.

The decision was not an easy one but the BJP decided to take it. Over nine months after the Kutch earthquake, on 7 October 2001, Narendra Modi assumed office as the CM of Gujarat.

The redevelopment of Kutch was CM Modi's first assignment as the CM. He was not even an MLA at that time. However, the decades that he had spent among people would hold him in good stead. It was hardly a time to celebrate. Narendra Modi, as the new CM, had his task cut out. He chose the redevelopment of Kutch as his top priority.

The painful scenes at Kutch were not the first time where he witnessed the effects of a calamity. As mentioned in the previous chapter, he was one of the first responders in Morbi. Also, he devoted several months in Kutch for relief before becoming the CM. He had experience in leading teams of dedicated volunteers to assist the administrative efforts. However, as CM, his efforts were no longer supplementary in nature.

Chief Minister Narendra Modi was now at the head of Gujarat's administrative machinery that faced manifold challenges. The initial rescue and relief effort had happened in the days following the earthquake and the administration now needed to tackle the medium and long-term effects of the calamity.

A multitude of problems stared the new CM in the face. For instance, the physical infrastructure had crumbled; the economy of Kutch was in a shambles and there was a dire need for the rebuilding of Kutch; vulnerable sections such as the elderly, pregnant women and children were among the worst sufferers and thousands were in a helpless condition; employment and the livelihoods of the people were destroyed; resources were to be provided to those on the brink of poverty; there was still the need to make the state resilient; the destroyed infrastructure such as schools and colleges was needed to be restored and made functional again.

After assuming the position of CM, Narendra Modi's approach to relief and rehabilitation work in Kutch was characterized by speed, efficiency and transparency. Decisions were made swiftly, ensuring that the recovery process moved forward rapidly. Under his leadership, there was a clear focus on future planning, vision and meticulous strategizing to achieve the desired outcomes. He set a target of three years for the entire rehabilitation and redevelopment of Kutch.

Many in Gujarat as well as outside remember the manner in which CM Modi went about accomplishing his work to this day. He was not keen on work that would look good on files. The focus was on work on ground.

Ramji Meriya, a Kutch-based reporter, recounts that CM Modi's governance was not about working in the cosy confines of the CM's office in the state capital, Gandhinagar. 'Chobari village in Bachau taluka was the epicentre of the earthquake. There was unimaginable destruction. In my village alone, 555 people died. Everything crashed. Not even a two-feet high wall could survive,' recalls Meriya.

The mood of the entire area was glum and sombre. They were living in utmost misery. The people came to know that the new CM, Narendra Modi would come and spend time with them for Diwali.

'He reached Chobari around 9.00–10.00 a.m. The mood was gloomy as most had lost someone close. Still, everyone gathered around for CM Modi,' recalls Meriya. CM Modi met every member of the village. He made it a point to visit every poor household. He also prayed at the temple of the village. He wanted to assure the people that his government was there for each one of them.

A local journalist asked CM Modi why he had decided to visit the small village on Diwali. 'The whole nation is lighting the diyas of Deepavali, but people from this village have lost family members. So I wish to be with them,' the CM replied. He told the people that he will make sure that Kutch rebuilt after the earthquake will be different from the one before.

When it was time for him to depart the village, he shared a message with the villagers, emphasizing the importance of moving forward and embracing the future. Aapda me Avsar—Meriya first heard of it from CM Modi when he visited Chobari during Diwali.

Chief Minister Narendra Modi even asked his council of ministers to spend their next Diwali in Kutch, to visit every earthquake-affected area and meet people to learn about the situation. Not only ministers, top officials would also pay visits week after week to gauge the impact. Each minister visited several villages. This not only motivated the spirits of people but also ensured a real ground-level audit of the work progress.

The practical side of the relief, rehabilitation and reconstruction efforts following a disaster situation involves presence on the field, ignoring personal comfort. After the Morbi dam breach, Narendra Modi has stayed in the inundation-affected town for over two months forgetting every other preoccupation. As he worked to rebuild Kutch, he demanded the same from his team. Most understood the demand of the situation and happily acquiesced. Senior officers would travel to the country-side on their weekends trying to understand the needs of the people.

Teams of volunteers, social organizations, functionaries of global bodies, experts and many others also contributed whole-heartedly and with a purpose. However, Narendra Modi would often surprise many of them with his own commitment to the rather daunting task.

Amrutbhai Patel, who worked with him at the CM's office, remembers that Narendra Modi's first priority after becoming the CM was to speed up the earthquake rehabilitation programme. To achieve this, he traversed the area extensively as he reviewed and supervised the efforts.

Patel remembers that CM Modi kept up with his incredibly demanding schedule even during Navratri. During the nine days of worship, devout Modi, like many devout Hindus, observes *vrat* (fast). 'I remember, even at that time, Narendra Modi had kept his Navratri vrat. All of us were worried about him and we even advised him not to fast during such a peculiar time, but he dismissed all concerns,' says Patel. District officials would ask Patel what the CM would eat during his visit. Even they were stunned when Patel told them that he would not consume any food item. 'CM Modi only used to have a glass of warm water with lemon drops during his fast, so we used to keep a flask full of warm water, often added a few drops of honey,' he said.

It was visible to all that the chief minister was driven by a purpose. Patel recalls that during a meeting with officials, the CM Modi expressed what was driving him to focus on the task. 'On 26 January 2002, it will be a year since the earthquake hit us!

The rehabilitation work you'd be doing till that time is what the world would be noticing, we only have so much time on our hands. So, if you wish your work to have an effect and the world to notice the work you've done then you'd have to do your best in the time we have,' he told everyone, according to Patel. Chief Minister Narendra Modi wanted the world to witness the resilience of Gujarat.

'All the people present in the meetings were filled with such zeal because of the CM's guidance. He helped the people present in the meetings to prioritize what was important and pace up the policy-making decisions, because of which the work done till 26 January 2002 was tremendous,' says Patel.

It was not just the officials and relief workers CM motivated. The people of Kutch drew strength from his presence. He visited villages and interacted with people, taking measures to address the problems faced by them.

Former Gujarat chief secretary Anil Mukim remembers how CM Modi raised the spirits of people. 'On 26 January 2002, it had been a year since the Kutch earthquake. The CM was visiting the village most affected by earthquake. As he reached the village, the atmosphere was very subdued and sorrowful. They were paying respect to those who had lost lives in the earthquake. It was a big room with 40–50 people sitting in it. CM went and sat in the midst of the people in the room.'

CM Modi stayed quiet for some time. Then he closed his eyes and began praying. As Narendra Modi softly chanted 'Shree Ram, Jai Ram, Jai Jai Ram,' the people too joined him, tears rolling down their cheeks. A heartfelt tribute was being paid to those who passed away. Gradually, the sombre mood lightened and an air of optimism began to waft.

'Just with this, CM Modi was able to instil positivity that now, we have to move ahead in life. Words may not have had the desired effect but his gesture did,' says Mukim. He at the helm of affairs was one biggest factor that helped improve people's confidence. He could easily connect with people. He was one of their own.

KEY TAKEAWAY

Without proper implementation, even the most well-drawn plans are meaningless. Also, the biggest challenge before any authority while dealing with a disaster situation is ensuring that an accurate picture of ground-level situation is created for suitable action. By being available at ground zero and spending time with people, a leader may ensure that they know the happenings at the grassroots much better than what files would have communicated. It also helps in boosting the morale of the people, without which a post-disaster reconstruction programme cannot be successful.

PREPARING THE TEAM

Political leadership and bureaucracy often suffer from a unique mindset that some like to refer to as the predecessor–successor syndrome. Many leaders, when they join an organization, try to blame their predecessor for the problems they face. Often, they begin by revamping the existing set-up or drawing plans anew.

However, in a scenario like Kutch, time was of the essence. CM Modi focussed his energy towards action. He told the officials that plans were already in place and it was the implementation that was most important.

Thiruppugazh, a Gujarat-cadre Indian Administrative Service (IAS) officer, was a senior officer in the state government, who also steered the Gujarat State Disaster Management Authority (GSDMA) formed after the earthquake. 'The greatest aspect of CM Modi was that he did not waste time. He did not wait to make a new policy. He said that the policy is already in place and let's implement it,' says Thiruppugazh.

As a social worker, Narendra Modi would work without a break seven days a week. He continued doing it as Gujarat's CM. He was intimately familiar with the entire state of Gujarat. He now expected every measure to have impact at the grassroots level. Naturally, the entire state machinery had to pull its socks up. Seven working days became a new normal. Emphasis was laid on better coordination between different departments. The only point of focus was timely implementation of plans.

The Narendra Modi government in Gujarat stood out for a unique aspect—faster decision-making. Not only did he take speedy decisions, he also inculcated a culture where time was not wasted.

Maheshwar Sahu, another bureaucrat who worked with the GSDMA recalls that CM as the chairperson of authority stressed on speedy execution. 'He gave us a deadline of less than three years, and the system delivered. Kutch became one of the fastest disaster reconstruction programmes in the world.'

As a volunteer, Narendra Modi had worked with government agencies during relief efforts. He was aware of many of the shortcomings of the bureaucratic processes. As CM, he sought to overcome them.

Varesh Sinha, former chief secretary of Gujarat says that CM Modi made two things clear: one, he would support every people-friendly initiative; two, he was willing to learn if someone had the requisite expertise. He was always available and willing to discuss and communicate.

Bureaucracy often gets blamed for red-tapism and ad-hocism. However, the key aspect often missed is that officers are only doing the bidding of those wielding political power. The same set of civil servants working under CM Modi became an incredibly responsive unit. 'He was always eager to learn. He knew a lot. Yet, he always showed that he wanted to learn about departments, the nitty-gritty of their functioning and more,' says Sinha.

Sinha recounts that the interest CM took in issues discussed during what were considered routine meetings came as a surprise. One of the first meetings called by him that Sinha also attended went on from 9.00 a.m. till 9.00 p.m. The CM and other officers brainstormed ideas for rebuilding Kutch. 'I noticed during the session that CM Modi did not speak much and listened to everybody,' says Sinha.

Without announcement or fanfare, Narendra Modi was ushering in a different and more work-oriented culture. He had, in his style, made known that he meant business. No aspect of governance was going to be casual. Decisions taken in meetings were converted into 'Government Orders'. This brought a sense of greater seriousness among all the officers, says Sinha.

There was some confusion in the system, created by a disoriented bureaucracy during the initial days. The first thing CM Modi did was to streamline the bureaucracy, make it accountable and put the system in tune with his goal of building a new Kutch.

'In one of the meetings, the CM was annoyed at the fact that whenever he asked for a secretary, he got the reply that they are busy with either Kutch-related work or visiting affected areas. He immediately announced that all the secretaries will travel to the affected areas on Friday and return by Monday. They were allocated specific areas. He even set timelines,' says Sinha.

CM Modi also added that all the earthquake-related issues were to be solved by the end of January 2002. Sinha was allotted Morbi. 'On Fridays, we used to travel and conduct Lok Darbar as directed by the CM,' he adds.

The CM had a habit of following up on every task he assigned. Soon, it became clear to everyone that the CM would eventually follow up on any task that he assigned, sometimes even after a month or two. Every officer realized that it was better to perform rather than be seen as someone who is not capable.

A former IAS officer of the Gujarat cadre, A.K. Sharma, worked with Narendra Modi when he was the CM and then as additional secretary in the Prime Minister's Office (PMO). He was assigned duty in the Lakhpat tehsil of Kutch.

'After becoming CM, Narendra Modi formed teams of around 25 IAS and IPS officers and allotted them tehsils in the affected districts. He also delegated power to those officials to tackle the problems in these tehsils. We collected feedback from the officers on a weekly basis and gave a report to the CM,' says Sharma. Whatever bottlenecks or problems emerged during the analysis of the feedback would be resolved by the CM. Sharma says that CM's decentralization of power led to faster recovery.

To streamline the process, new authorities were established in Bhuj, Anjar, Rapar, Bachao and Gandhidham. Collector-level officials were stationed in each tehsil, along with officers from the District Development Office (DDO). These officials were assigned specific areas of responsibility within each tehsil.

This decentralized approach enabled swift surveys to be conducted, ensuring that people could begin rebuilding their homes promptly. To conduct the necessary surveys, teams of engineers and officials visited every village, meticulously assessing the damage and documenting the requirements for reconstruction. Their surveys played a crucial role in ensuring that the necessary resources and manpower were allocated efficiently to each affected area.

Houses were classified into different categories based on the extent of damage caused. The government categorized areas (G1, G2, G3, G4, G5) according to the effects of the disaster to provide compensation to the affected people.

Monetary compensation was provided to many families. Also, the information collected during these surveys was used for taking informed, data-driven decisions.

At the district and local levels, CM Modi set up coordination committees comprising of government officials, local leaders and NGOs. These committees held regular meetings to monitor the progress of the relief work and to identify any gaps or challenges in the response plan.

KEY TAKEAWAY

The best way to make an unresponsive system work effectively is to delegate authority and also making those wielding it accountable. Results would themselves speak of the performance or the lack of it. Additionally, accurate data is useful in ensuring that specific support reaches the relevant sections in need.

Overall, CM's emphasis on monitoring and review helped to ensure that the relief and rescue work was being carried out efficiently and effectively, and that aid was reaching the people who needed it the most. It also demonstrated the importance of strong leadership and effective coordination in responding to disasters.

He conducted visits to the affected areas to personally assess the extent of the damage and ensure that relief and assistance were being provided to those who needed it the most. He also visited relief camps to interact with the affected people and get a first-hand understanding of their needs and concerns.

The winter was approaching, so he sensed that arranging temporary accommodation for the people was one of the priorities. He devised a comprehensive plan that involved providing temporary shelters in the form of tents to those who had lost their homes. To accommodate the looming winter, he recommended the construction of wooden houses as a practical solution. People were provided compensation to build temporary accommodation. He also prioritized the restoration of basic services such as water supply, electricity and transportation to ensure that the affected people could resume their normal lives as soon as possible.

Chapter 3

Kutch Bounces Back

THE TURNING POINT

Having set a smooth and clear working tone, Chief Minister Narendra Modi began the task of rebuilding Kutch. From infrastructure, livelihood concerns to education, there was a plethora of fronts on which his government had to work.

In December 2001, two months after Narendra Modi had taken over the Gujarat government, the Gujarat Earthquake Reconstruction and Rehabilitation Policy (GERRP) was released.[1] The policy document formed a comprehensive blueprint of the work to which the state government committed itself. In his foreword, Narendra Modi as CM underlined his commitment rather succinctly. 'Our grief is accompanied by our steadfast resolution. It was to rebuild Gujarat,' he said.[2]

Based on the policy, GERRP and the Gujarat Emergency Earthquake Reconstruction Project (GEERP) were launched. The objectives of the projects were aimed at addressing the gamut of challenges that the region faced.

The projects aimed at building and repairing houses, reviving local economy, improving education and health sectors, providing social protection for weaker sections, providing health and psychological support to the victims, restoring infrastructure, empowering women and supporting children.

In the longer term, the objectives were very clear. The policy aimed to improve disaster preparedness and emergency response capacity. It also sought to reduce vulnerability through long-term mitigation programmes. Multilateral organizations like the World Bank, the ADB, and so on, played crucial roles in the projects.

For every task, financial and other resources had to be generated. According to a UNDP report, Kutch bore 90 per cent of all deaths and about 85 per cent of all asset losses. Those in agriculture, livestock-rearing and salt production—the mainstays of the economy—suffered tremendous losses, as did the crafts sector, for which Kutch is renowned, a UNDP report said. Assessment of damage put the total direct losses state-wide at \$3.5 billion. The cost of reconstruction is estimated at \$2.5 billion, held the UNDP report.[3]

Narendra Modi began forming teams to focus on specific problems. Those with required expertise were given prominent roles. One of the key individuals involved in the rebuilding of Kutch was Anil Das, who, as the project implementation officer of the ADB, made significant contribution towards the rehabilitation efforts. Das provided detailed insights into how Kutch recovered under CM Modi's leadership.

There are many aspects to the Kutch Rehabilitation Programme. One of them is the period before Narendra Modi's arrival, during which fundamental policies took shape, such as the Housing Rehabilitation Programme under Keshubhai Patel and the setting up of the GSDMA. While this policy was agreed upon in principle, it took time to materialize, says Das. 'After CM Modi's arrival, effect of the policies started taking shape. He didn't change the policies, but gave a new vision to the programme,' he states.

Even though he was new to being a CM, Narendra Modi Modi took various important decisions that had long-term objectives. For him, the entire endeavour was not just about helping Kutch get back on its feet but also about building a new Kutch in sync with his philosophy of Aapda me Avsar.

The Gujarat government followed a systematic multi-step approach to solve the housing issue. Firstly, it prioritized removing the rubble and debris. Following this, the interim shelters were set up for the immediate relief. Then, the government focused on the reconstruction and restoration of the collapsed and demolished houses. Simultaneously, the damaged units were repaired, and the undamaged were retrofitted, respectively. Finally, the government led to the rebuilding of social and community infrastructure to facilitate the recovery and restoration of affected communities.

Narendra Modi tried to bring innovation to the construction of houses and other infrastructure, based on a futuristic vision. He did not want to simply borrow and duplicate previous models, including the Latur model, says Maheshwar Sahu. He motivated officials to learn from models, including past experiences of nations like Japan and develop their own model for Kutch, relying on innovation, technology and futuristic approaches.

He insisted on earthquake-resistant buildings, even if they would take longer to be constructed. Eminent experts from around the globe were roped in. One of them was an IIT (Indian Institute of Technology) Roorkee professor, A.S. Arya, who led the Earthquake Reconstruction Programme. The teams conducted various tests to ensure that the houses being rebuilt were resistant to earthquakes.

'There was a Shake Table Test. In this test, constructed models were subjected to full pressure with the help of a tractor to gauge the impact. There were two models—one was a general construction, and the other model complied with the codes for earthquake resistance. Through this, one was able to look at the visual aspect of how the impact works,' says Das, who was impressed by Narendra Modi's focus on planning and not taking shortcuts.

'The quake-hit areas are being built using world-class technology to provide a better living environment. After reconstruction work is completed, they will look like modern, twenty-first-century townships,' CM Modi told his team.

Rajib Shaw, a professor in Japan, was part of the rehabilitation project. He was in constant contact with CM Modi throughout the Kutch rehabilitation work. Shaw says, 'I remember my first meeting with CM where we discussed the Kobe earthquake in Japan. His in-depth knowledge of the Kobe earthquake and its rehabilitation efforts was truly impressive. He emphasized that disaster risk reduction involves more than just science and engineering; it requires a multidisciplinary approach, encompassing social sciences, economics, geography, urban planning and various other disciplines. It was rare to witness leaders of his stature engage in such detailed discussions on technical matters.'

Narendra Modi had made it clear to Shaw and others that the reconstruction efforts also had to focus on the potential for future disasters, ensuring that buildings were designed to be multi-hazard resilient.

'So, Professor K.S. Arya and our team decided to create an experimental model. We constructed two half-sized buildings on a shake table in Radhanpur, Gujarat. One building followed standard construction practices, while the other incorporated retrofitting elements. Japanese engineers were invited to assess the impact of shaking during the experiment, which was conducted in the presence of local masons. This allowed us to observe the collapse dynamics and determine necessary measures. Subsequently, we provided training to local masons to equip them with the knowledge to construct earthquake-resistant homes,' adds Shaw.

A range of seismic-safe design and construction technologies were explored, including considerations for cyclone resistance in the construction of new houses. Time-tested traditional building techniques like 'Bhongas', mud houses preferred by a significant portion of the tribal population, were also promoted.

'Chief Minister Narendra Modi stressed that houses must be constructed to withstand any potential disaster. He also advocated for the expansion of roads and streets in villages to facilitate easy evacuation,' recalls Dollarray Gor, a BJP leader from Rapar in Kutch.

The ADB 2008 completion report titled *India: Gujarat Earthquake Rehabilitation and Reconstruction Project* highlights the government's approach to futuristic and disaster-resilient construction. Most of the public–private partnership houses were built in situ with multi-hazard resistant technology after extensive consultation with beneficiaries. Masons and engineers were trained in multi-hazard resistant housing construction and reconstruction. These houses are registered under the joint ownership of the husband and wife and have been insured. Compared to the pre-earthquake situation, the quality of construction has improved, houses are larger, and the proportion of houses with separate toilets has doubled (to 64%).[4]

As the report indicates, the Gujarat government under Chief Minister Narendra Modi emphasized on innovative processes, including earthquake-resistant construction. It also mentions in-situ construction and owner-driven construction policy. CM believed that people should have a say in the type of house they wanted to rebuild and its location. Typically, after disasters, individuals often lack the opportunity to make such choices, especially in cases of significant displacement. It was no easy task. After all, over 3,00,000 houses were to be built or repaired.

'CM Modi proposed the idea of offering people a wide range of options from which they could choose, and these choices would be incorporated into their individual financing agreements and arrangements with the government. The fundamental concept behind this approach was "build back better",' says Das.

The two key policy elements in CM Modi's initiative to reconstruct villages and towns in Kutch were the owner-driven process and hazard-resistant construction. The reconstruction also focussed on a minimal relocation approach, favouring in-situ construction.

People welcomed the ideas proposed by the government, as they could sense the sincerity behind the efforts. Community leaders actively participated in the decision-making process, including the selection of construction sites. A significant majority of Gram Sabhas passed resolutions expressing their strong desire not to relocate but to rebuild their houses on the existing sites.

Finally, over 90 per cent of the construction occurred in-situ, resulting in minimal relocation.[5] This marked a groundbreaking achievement for any government following a disaster. Studies have shown that relocation and the grid housing format for rehabilitation had certain social impacts after the 1993 Latur earthquake in Maharashtra.[6] Kutch stands as a successful example of rehabilitation without disturbing the region's social fabric.

Instead of adhering to conventional procedures that involve contractors in construction, the chief minister advocated for owner-driven construction. This marked the first-ever implementation of owner-driven reconstruction in such a large-scale rehabilitation effort. People were even provided with the option to choose the design of their houses.

Overall, the decentralization of authority and active community participation in the relief and rehabilitation efforts following the Kutch earthquake helped foster trust and confidence in the government's approach based on owner-driven construction.

The CM also ensured that the new houses were constructed in the names of both husbands and wives. This simple gesture aimed to promote female ownership of property and gained greater acceptance among families.

Gujarat government officials held meetings with over 10 lakh householders. Though cumbersome, it helped educate people about the process of building houses. The government conducted technical audits through organizations like the National Council for Cement and Building Materials (NCCBM), Central Building Research Institute (CBRI), etc. It also ensured the availability of raw material through numerous outlets. More than 6.5 lakh bank accounts were opened in a few months as all the payments were processed through banks to ensure transparency.[7]

There was also a shortage of trained engineers to build large-scale dwellings. It was suggested that technical students could be allowed to take part in the rehabilitation–rebuilding process. CM Modi endorsed the idea. As a result, 3,000–4,000 young ITI (Industrial Training Institute) students and their professors were involved with the work.

Needless to say, to meet the requirements of the large-scale construction, a commensurate manpower was also needed. Workers were brought from least affected districts like Godhra, Panchmahal and also from outside Gujarat. Skilled workers such as electricians and plumbers were also brought in from different locations. Without their presence, the reconstruction work would have been inordinately delayed. Narendra Modi, who mobilized hundreds of volunteers for the Morbi floods as an RSS pracharak or handled thousands of party workers as a political leader, knew well how to fill the gaps in manpower requirements.

'Ninety per cent of the houses were constructed within a year and a half,' says Das. Not only were quality, hazard-resistant houses constructed in a speedy manner, but they were also insured. 'Narendra Modi took mass insurance for all the houses that were constructed,' says Das. Leading insurance companies were roped in to provide insurance to the houses against various risks.

CM Modi made it clear that for one year, priority should be given to enhancing awareness among the people about earthquake resistance. Thus, the Gujarat government also put in huge efforts to spread awareness about the reconstruction, especially regarding the need for earthquake-resistant buildings and owner-driven construction. To raise awareness about the novel strategies of constructing earthquake-resistant in-situ houses, as well as to promote owner-driven construction, extensive publicity drives and campaigns were conducted. Whether it be buses or hoardings, everything had advertisements on the basics of quake-resistant construction. 'There were a variety of earthquake resistant housing design options that were made available, a large number of engineers and masons were trained for it. For example, putting bands at various levels of construction was linked to the payment of three instalments of housing compensation. This also added to large scale awareness about earthquake resistant elements,' says Nidhi Prabha Tewari, a social sector expert who worked in the Kutch rehabilitation programme as head of the camp office of GSDMA.

Tata Sumo vans with LCD projectors would travel from village to village, where they would exhibit a film in which a popular actor would narrate the basic ideas behind earthquake-resilient and owner-driven construction. Entire villages would turn up to watch the film.

KEY TAKEAWAY

Disaster rehabilitation and rebuilding present an opportunity to 'build back better' and incorporate future disaster resilience into the reconstruction process. It necessitates an innovative and forward-looking approach.

FUTURE-READY PUBLIC INFRASTRUCTURE

The foundation of the Kutch model of redevelopment was CM Modi's belief in finding long-term solutions. The Gujarat team relied on expertise, either local or global, to create the best possible infrastructure. It was not a patch-up job. Kutch was being rebuilt to sustain itself. As a sound depiction of CM Modi's Aapda me Avsar philosophy, Kutch was not just being rebuilt but also reimagined. For him, this was also an opportunity to create a new Kutch with better infrastructure, roads, sewerage and other facilities. He focused on 'build back better' approach. Urban planners and developers were roped in to create better cities, given the seismic zone and the possibility of future earthquakes.

Bhuj Area Development Authority (BHADA) was constituted to execute the new plans. A comprehensive and detailed plan was prepared to expand the otherwise congested and thickly populated Bhuj city.

Experts often point out how congested lanes proved fatal in times of calamity. Over 300 children and teachers were crushed in Anjar during the Kutch earthquake due to buildings collapsing on them from both sides.[8] Even in other disasters, congested streets create problems as fire tenders and rescue teams find it difficult to move forward. Chief Minister Narendra Modi ensured that the new infrastructure created did not suffer from these drawbacks. Bhuj city saw a fourfold expansion in the area after the reconstruction work was over. An extensive road network was built. Usually, town planning and rebuilding takes years to get completed, but Bhuj is an example of fast, efficient and futuristic town replanning and rebuilding. The towns of Bhachau, Rapar, Anjar also expanded and transformed in a planned way. This is one of the major reasons why Kutch rehabilitation stands out as a disaster management model. The rebuilding programme gave way to addressing the issues faced by people and building new public infrastructure.

Roads were widened extensively, and drinking water systems were established with extensive pipe connections. Bhuj and other towns, which could hardly boast of a modern sewage system, got one. Earlier, women used to spend around 8–10 hours fetching drinking water. Sometimes, drinking water was provided to them from water tankers once every five–six days. The river basin grid was developed so that Narmada River's water could reach most parts of Kutch.

Bhavnaben Ruparel, a resident of Kutch, bears testimony to the turn for the better that life took for many survivors. The pain they underwent was impossible to assuage, but the focus on infrastructure after the devastation brought some much-needed improvements.

'We used to fill water from tankers. Everyday, ladies and kids would take buckets in their hands and fill water for their daily usage. Every Gram Sabha of Gujarat would receive 10,000 litres of water each day and it was a huge expense for the government. To solve this problem, Narendra Modi established pipelines from Narmada to every household,' Bhavnaben says. Now, the whole of Gujarat drinks Narmada's water.

The rebuilt Kutch not only had a better availability of potable water but also had a better sanitation system. An unexpected benefit of the construction of the new houses was that the number of residences with attached toilets also saw a rise.

A key area that needed to be focussed on was the condition of schools. As a leader, Narendra Modi always stressed on quality education. Even as his administration worked on other pressing demands, this vital area did not go unaddressed. Children going back to school would lend normalcy to the affected zone. For that, the state administration chalked out a plan. Thousands of primary school rooms needed to be repaired. Many schools were built using funding from diverse sources.

In a recent speech, Prime Minister Narendra Modi recalled, 'Krantiguru Shyamji Krishna Verma University was formed in 2003 in Kutch. At the same time more than 35 new colleges have also been established. Moreover, more than 1,000 new schools were built in such a short time. The district hospital of Kutch was completely destroyed in the earthquake. Today Kutch has a modern earthquake resistant hospital; and more than 200 new medical centres are functioning.'[9]

Hundreds of government office buildings were also repaired or reconstructed and built into modern infrastructure, and the electricity infrastructure was revamped. A new irrigation network was built as well.

The medical infrastructure had also been badly damaged. Many of the health services, however, resumed soon after the earthquake, albeit in temporary or semi-permanent buildings. The Narendra Modi government also undertook the task of creating the best medical infrastructure, including hospitals, primary and community health centres.

KEY TAKEAWAY

The concept of Aapda me Avsar stands as one of the most effective disaster management strategies for any nation or community facing challenging times. It not only enhances the management of the calamity at hand but also fosters preparedness for the future. For example, while the response to Covid-19 has led to the development of a robust mechanism for handling endemic or pandemic situations in India, the rehabilitation efforts following the Kutch earthquake shaped a new and improved Kutch, with enhanced infrastructure and a better quality of life for its people.

JAN BHAGIDARI: COMMUNITY PARTICIPATION FOR A NEW KUTCH

While Aapda me Avsar served as the guiding principle behind CM Modi's model of Kutch disaster management and reconstruction, the most fundamental aspect of this approach was to secure active participation from the people in the entire process.

Narendra Modi, who had extensive experience working with people as an organizer, initially in the social organization, the RSS and later with the BJP, had a deep understanding of the inherent strength of India's community life.

People's power can achieve anything, more so in a disaster scenario where government and other systems play the role of facilitators while the will of the people drives the community back to normalcy. CM Modi was not only aiming at normalcy but also to positively use the situation for building a new, more resilient Kutch.

'Owner-driven construction is the hallmark of the Kutch redevelopment model. It was a result of Narendra Modi's approach of Jan Bhagidari in the rehabilitation work. CM Modi laid emphasis on community participation. For instance, there was a need for infrastructure expansion, but the challenge was land acquisition. He successfully conveyed to the people the importance of expanding the cities of Bhuj and others, leading to voluntary land contributions from the community,' says Anil Das.

'After witnessing the success of the Shake Table Test, CM Modi told us that it should not remain limited to laboratories but should be demonstrated to the people of Kutch. It was crucial for them to understand how and why disaster relief infrastructure should be,' recalls Rajib Shaw.

The government formed people's committees at the local level, which included representatives from various stakeholders, including the *sarpanch* (village head), local NGOs and community members. A three-tier arrangement—the village committee, the District Advisory Committee and the State Advisory Committee—formed the structure for the redevelopment work. These committees played a crucial role in conveying the needs and requirements of the affected population to the government and coordinating relief efforts at the grassroots level. The involvement of village heads and other community representatives in relief and rehabilitation efforts ensured accurate assessment and response to the needs of those affected. The government also provided training and support to these committees.

Overall, decentralization and community participation were key to the success of relief and rehabilitation efforts after the Kutch earthquake. These principles built trust and confidence in the government's disaster response capabilities. They also ensured that relief efforts were customized to the unique needs of affected communities, facilitating timely recovery and rehabilitation.

Large public meetings were organized in Bhuj, Bachao and other places. Senior officials, MLAs and community leaders addressed them. These gatherings aimed to raise awareness and promote community participation in urban development initiatives.

Narendra Modi also ensured that there was a balance of power and empowerment among various stakeholders like government departments, local government wings, community groups, NGOs, international bodies like the ADB, etc. No single entity was allowed to dictate the direction, says Anil Das. This often is a hindrance in disaster management efforts, which can make the process lopsided. However, at the same time, the CM also ensured the accountability of each stakeholder.

Experts have often highlighted systemic misgovernance, which can lead to the exploitation of the poor during challenging times. The effectiveness of a policy depends on both intent and implementation. A well-crafted plan on paper can prove ineffective in practice.

A major, yet often unstated, accomplishment for CM Modi was that he was able to keep a stringent check on corruption during Kutch's reconstruction. Managing the flow of funds and materials from government, NGOs and other organizations is a major challenge during disaster relief efforts, with considerable scope for leakage and corruption. Modi consistently urged authorities to monitor and take strict action against corruption. A Talathi was sacked by the chief minister for corruption in the Kutch rehabilitation work.

Narendra Modi ensured that the whole system was leakage-free. As the PM, too, he has successfully demonstrated that the famous problem stated by former PM Rajiv Gandhi about massive leakages can be addressed through technology and banking systems. At the centre, PM Modi's government post 2014 has opened millions of accounts under Jan Dhan Yojana and opted for Direct Benefit Transfers (DBT) to the account of the needy to tackle the challenge of systemic leakage.

During the Kutch rehabilitation process as well, he relied on banking systems. Most of the payments were made only through banks. Accounts were opened on a large scale. Officials recall that huge quantities of new passbooks were printed and brought from other states.

KEY TAKEAWAY

Active community participation is vital for a successful and expeditious disaster management process.

DATA-BACKED PLAN

One of the features of CM Modi's governance model is his scientific approach, backed by data and information. Coordination and data-driven planning were important pillars of Kutch rebuilding.

Communication systems had collapsed in Kutch, and the lack of information was a challenge for relief as well as planning of rehabilitation. By gathering data from the ground, he was able to get a better understanding of the situation and to identify gaps or challenges in the relief efforts. This helped him to make necessary adjustments to the response plan and to ensure that relief and assistance were reaching the people who needed it the most.

Nidhi Tewari was part of the information dissemination and coordination process. She says, 'In the beginning, there was no data of the level of damage. First, survey teams were sent out in the field and data on damage was collected and organized. Compensations was based on the level of damage suffered by houses. Given the scale of data, computerisation was introduced for the first time at block and taluk government offices so that easy access and transparency could be ensured.'

CM Modi wanted an information gathering and dispensation

mechanism. An innovative mechanism called 'Setu' was established with the help of NGOs like Abhiyan. Setu centres and kiosks were established at various locations in Kutch. At a time when social media was absent, they acted as the information bridge between the government and people.

This sharing of information was one of the crucial parts of the Kutch Redevelopment Plan. The Rehabilitation Information Management System (RIMS) was created, integrating information gathered through Setu and available data with government agencies.[10]

Narendra Modi has a great passion for technology. In those days, remote sensing and satellite images were used for monitoring the progress of the redevelopment. Extensive use of the Geographic Information System (GIS) mapping technology was done. A database based on the GIS was developed. The GIS and RIMS were linked, and dynamic maps were created.

Therefore, the data and information collected from the field, with the assistance of volunteers and technology, formed the foundation of the rehabilitation and reconstruction efforts in Kutch.

GSDMA: POLICY AND LEGAL FRAMEWORK OF RESILENCE

Gujarat was the first Indian state to push an Act establishing a policy and legal framework for disaster management. In 2002, CM Modi announced the GSDM policy. The state was the pioneer in adopting a disaster policy. It helped in framing the right strategies and defining the roles of each stakeholders.

Soon in 2003, the GSDM Act came into force after being passed by the state assembly. It was a precursor to the National Disaster Management Act (NDMA), which came into being only in 2005, along with the establishment of the NDMA. The law was made after a thorough study of similar legislations across the globe and extensive discussions with several stakeholders. It is one of the robust legislative frameworks in the world, offering a wide scope of strategies for disaster management. Hundreds of legal awareness camps were conducted for people.

CM Modi made Gujarat ready to handle disasters better in the future, which is discussed in detail in the next chapter. The GSDMA framework provided the base to build the structure on it.

The GSDMA was established in 2001, which became the nodal agency to coordinate all disaster management activities in the state. This helped in smooth coordination between various stakeholders involved in Kutch relief and rehabilitation. The GSDMA, headed by the CM, not only acted as a strong enabler for Kutch earthquake management but also preparing Gujarat for any future disasters.

Maheshwar Sahu recalls what CM Modi told the officials, 'After the rehabilitation, people should forget the tears and feel that they got a better life. The GSDMA should strive to achieve this and make Kutch model an example for not just the nation, but the world to follow.'

The core philosophy of Narendra Modi's disaster management approach, such as preparing communities for disasters, transforming challenges into opportunities and involving the people, are readily evident in the GSDM Act and the strategies employed by the GSDMA. The objectives of the authority involves 'promoting awareness', 'preparing the community', 'increasing capacity to deal with potential disasters' and 'being a repository of information concerning disaster management'.[11] It shows the vision of Narendra Modi as early as in 2002, during his initial days as an administrator.

The Gujarat Institute of Disaster Management (GIDM) was set up, becoming the central authority for disaster learning, developing futuristic management techniques, stakeholder training and compiling valuable information on disaster management strategies. Today, GIDM has risen to the status of a centre of global recognition.

KEY TAKEAWAY

A robust legislative and policy framework is essential for effective disaster management. Gujarat serves as a role model for establishing such a strong framework supported by institutions like the GSDMA, preventing the disaster management process from derailing.

REBUILDING LIVES, REIMAGINING ECONOMY

Disaster effects range from the damage done to physical and durable assets to the changes in economic flows. While devastation occur the moment the disaster strikes, some effects come into play over a period of time.

At the individual level, disasters may impact the ability of households to earn incomes. At sectoral levels, it may lead to a significant reduction in the production of goods or services. This has a bearing at the macro-economic level as well. The remedy for a region struggling to get back on its feet after having faced a disaster cannot be in terms of physical infrastructure alone.

The rehabilitation efforts can be holistic only if they are thoroughly focussed on the human element, including economic aspects. After the Kutch earthquake, a key aspect that had to be looked into was the restoration of people's livelihoods. Many of the survivors are themselves capable of rebuilding their lives. However, they need systemic support to get their lives back on track. One of the first tasks that can be assigned is providing people with employment.

Narendra Modi, as the CM of Gujarat, decided to reimagine the scenario and drew long-term measures that can not only generate thousands of jobs but also boost the economy of Kutch. The reconstruction projects were mandated not only for rehabilitation but also to restore local industries; assist artisans, farmers, etc.; and regenerate livelihoods.

The government rolled out an incentive plan, providing tax relief to thousands of industrial units which had stopped functioning due to the earthquake. Tax-free loans and financial assistance were provided to industries, artisans, shop owners, etc. Farmers were given input kits with seeds, fertilizers, tools and so on. Masons got a significant opportunity in the rebuilding of houses and buildings. A massive self-employment scheme for women was also launched.

Chief Minister Narendra Modi took the initiative to resolve disputes related to pension schemes. He found that pension scheme-related cases for amounts as little as a few hundred rupees had been dragging on for decades. The state's finance secretary was asked to look into the matter. Hundreds of cases were resolved in no time, and people received what was their due in the most critical of times.

He knew the potential of Kutch and believed it could become an economic powerhouse. He focussed on bringing investments and converting Kutch into an industrial hub. 'One area where CM Modi saw huge opportunity was to make Kutch an industrial zone. After the earthquake, new industries came in, leading to employment generation. For instance, the company Welspun came in and 11,000 people got employment. Today it has a huge steel industry. People from all across the country now come here for employment,' says former bureaucrat A.K. Sharma, who worked closely with CM Modi.

Along with work, Narendra Modi always focussed on

communication. He believed that the right message should reach the right person. He wanted the world to know that Kutch was rising. He also wanted the industry and businesses to know that Kutch was now a desirable destination.

'In January 2002, Narendra Modi convened a meeting in Delhi with several ambassadors from various nations to India. A presentation was given in front of them on the work being done in the Kutch. The image of a shattered Kutch was replaced with those of a developing area,' adds Sharma.

Narendra Modi understood that to usher in prosperity in the devastated Kutch, the role of industry would be vital. So, he did not just offer tax benefits. He offered them a conducive climate in which businesses could grow. He became the ambassador for Kutch and actively sought investments.

Leading business personality Balkrishan Goenka, managing director of Welspun group, which is into textiles, says that it was CM Modi who urged them to consider expanding in Kutch. 'I expressed my hesitation at first, highlighting the challenges posed by the devastating earthquake. I mentioned the lack of basic amenities such as water, electricity and roads, as well as the daunting task of establishing a large-scale plant in such circumstances. However, CM Modi confidently stated that Kutch holds immense potential, and investing just ₹1 would yield returns of $1. His message was delivered with utmost seriousness and conviction, leaving no doubt in my mind that he genuinely spoke from the heart. Inspired, I moved forward with the project in Kutch,' says Goenka.

Moreover, as the CM of Gujarat, Narendra Modi decided to make Kutch tax-free for five years.[12] Many companies came and the people of Kutch got the means of employment.[13] Imports and exports from the Kandla and Mandvi Port surged. Today, Kutch has all segments of the industry including power, steel, cement, chemicals, textiles and food processing, along with traditional handicrafts and salt.

Former additional chief secretary of Gujarat Rajiv Gupta says that Narendra Modi also focussed on agriculture in the area. 'He gave importance to agriculture. For instance, he implemented a plan for cultivating dragon fruit, naming it Kamalam. He knew that there could be a higher production of fruit in Kutch. Today, there is so much dragon fruit production in this area that the farmers earn well,' says Gupta.

Funding is essential for any post-disaster recovery and rebuilding efforts. There are multilateral organizations like the ADB, World Bank, governments and philanthropic donors as well as the option of crowdfunding that can be used to generate the required funds. However, the economic loss caused by calamities can be so huge that even multiple sources of funding may still leave a lot to be desired. It is important that post-disaster rebuilding activity also focusses on the potential of the affected region to attract investment.

According to a UNDP report after the Kutch earthquake, the assessment of damage statewide hovered around \$3.5 billion. The cost of reconstruction was estimated at \$2.5 billion. 'Those in agriculture, livestock-rearing and salt production—the mainstays of the economy—suffered tremendous losses, as did the crafts sector, for which Kachch (Kutch) is renowned.'[14]

There are different ways to assess damage, but they all point to one thing—the quintessential requirement of funds, including investment. Investment decisions are, however, based on the cold logic of the probability of making reasonably robust returns. The Gujarat administration sought to utilize all sources of funding.

Not just bureaucrats, even the common people could sense the purpose behind the rehabilitation efforts. A farmer, Dilipbhai Dungariya, says that initially they felt that it would take 40–50 years to recover everything. 'A few months after the earthquake, Narendra Modi assumed the role of Chief Minister of Gujarat. It was seen that his focus was on redevelopment of Kutch. His dedicated efforts led to significant development in Kutch within just two–three years. Furthermore, the arrival of Narmada water in the region proved highly advantageous for both farmers like me and factories,' he says.

Years later, in a speech as the Prime Minister, Narendra Modi said, 'Today, Kutch has the world's largest cement plants. In welded-pipe production, Kutch ranks second globally. The world's second-largest textile plant is in Kutch. Also, Asia's first Special Economic Zone (SEZ) was set up in Kutch. Kandla and Mundra ports, collectively handle 30 per cent of country's (shipping) cargo. Over 30 per cent of India's salt is produced in Kutch. The dream that we saw for Kutch during 2001-02 in those adverse situations, is now a reality in front of your eyes.'[15]

Narendra Modi adopted a 360-degree approach when it came to developing Kutch. A vital aspect was the focus on tourism. He decided to rebuild the area in a sustainable manner. The development had to be anchored in the region's natural strengths, and one of its strengths was its breathtaking natural beauty. Hence, he focussed on the region's tourism potential.

A cohesive vision that would allow Kutch to emerge as a bright spot on the global tourism map had been missing before 2001. Infrastructure was created while information was also made readily available for the benefit of potential tourists. There are several resorts in Kutch today. People have even converted their traditional mud houses or *bhungas* into homestays, which is a popular option among tourists now.

'Things changed. People could now stay at the homes of the locals and hotel revenues also increased. Petrol pumps were set up, handicrafts got a boost and women were able to become financially stable, thanks to the vision of Narendra Modi,' says Miya Hussain, the sarpanch of Dhordo, a village in the Rann.

Rann Utsav, the internationally renowned cultural festival that takes place in the White Rann, the vast salt desert in Kutch, was initiated to unlock the region's tourism potential and boost the local economy. Showcasing the region's rich cultural heritage and promoting the skills of local artisans and craftsmen, it played a major role in the transformation of Kutch.

A tent city was established for tourists in Dhordo, a remote village located adjacent to the White Rann, where the annual Rann Utsav is held. Under the visionary leadership of the then Chief Minister, Narendra Modi, Dhordo evolved from an isolated village into a thriving tourism destination. It went on to earn the prestigious title of 'Best Tourism Village' from the World Tourism Organization.[16]

CM Modi invited superstar Amitabh Bachchan to become the face of the campaign. The renowned actor made the punchline, '*Kutch nahi dekha to kuch nahi dekha,*' incredibly popular.[17]

Singer Geetaben Rabari from Kutch is a household name in Gujarat. 'Because of Narendra Modi's hard work people, from my village got their houses back and also started earning their livelihoods,' she says. 'My singing career got a big boost in the initial days by the Rann Utsav,' Rabari adds. The festival provided musicians the chance to recreate their traditional music while also benefitting professionally.

KUTCHI PRIDE TAKES CENTRE STAGE

Narendra Modi not only tried to rebuild Kutch, he also tried to lend a sense of pride among the people who had seen such excruciating devastation. He built memorials as a tribute to their struggle.

Smriti Van, a memorial and museum in Bhuj, was built to commemorate all those who lost their lives in the earthquake. It is a symbol of the resilience of the people. Chief Minister Narendra Modi tried to tell the world about the importance of the fighting spirit of the people in times of the severest of calamities. The museum also has details of the Kutch earthquake and serves as a vast repository of information on disaster management models. The Veer Balak Smarak was constructed in Anjar in the memory of the children who died in the earthquake.

The fury of the earthquake had hardly left any buildings untouched. Kutch is a place of significant historical importance and boasts of several historical sites. It has connections to the Indus Valley Civilization. Many of the heritage buildings that suffered damages were also rebuilt, including Gurudwara Lakhpat Sahib.

The Gurudwara is associated with the travels of the revered founder of Sikhism, Guru Nanak Dev. According to locals, it is believed that Guru Nanak, during his visit to Mecca, had stayed at that place. Narendra Modi learned of the condition of the Gurudwara and felt that it should be reconstructed in the same manner as it was in ancient times, restoring its glory. He brought artisans from Rajasthan and Uttar Pradesh for this purpose. As a result, United Nations Educational, Scientific and Cultural Organization (UNESCO) awarded Gurudwara Lakhpat Sahib as the best-restored place of worship.[18]

THE TURNING POINT

Numerous studies and reports highlight the 2001 Kutch earthquake as a turning point that reshaped India's approach to natural and other disasters and its response to them.[19] There are several factors that contributed to this particular calamity becoming an inflection point.

First and foremost, the magnitude of the calamity was enormous. It raised great awareness, suggesting that the world had to come together to strengthen mechanisms, whether early warning systems or post-disaster relief. The world had already been working on developing a paradigm for improved disaster management throughout the last decade of twentieth century. In India, a significant difference that emerged was the shift of disaster management from the Agriculture Ministry to the more resource-rich Ministry of Home Affairs.

Following the earthquake, the state of Gujarat created a much more systematic mechanism to deal with calamities. Till the beginning of the twenty-first century, institutional lethargy had led to the continuation of a system where response to diverse calamities was marred by constants like inadequate resources and lack of clarity related to post-disaster roles even among institutional players. However, a more proactive and community-centric approach developed after the Kutch disaster. Senior bureaucrat and former Chief Executive Officer (CEO) of the GSDMA P.K. Mishra has provided a detailed account of the subject in his book *The Kutch Earthquake 2001: Recollections, Lessons and Insights.*

Mishra writes that in terms of both number and magnitude, the performance in respect to housing, restoration of physical and social infrastructure and livelihood regeneration is impressive. 'It is not limited to the reconstruction of physical assets. There is a focus on enabling the earthquake victims to earn their livelihood. There are important initiatives to enhance capability for disaster management. When compared with similar programmes elsewhere in the country and abroad, the performance of Gujarat has been considered spectacular,' Mishra states.

It was also a stepping stone to the future. The Kutch model is not only about the scale and complexity but also about preparing for the future and reimagining existing models. Kutch's response paved the path towards a more prepared future. Having laid the foundation for a prosperous Kutch, Narendra Modi moved towards creating a more prepared Gujarat. He introduced to the world a new paradigm of disaster management, based on innovation, community participation and preparedness.

Simultaneously, key developments were taking place at the national and global level for the creation of more prepared and resilient nations and communities.

Chapter 4

Mission Preparedness

THE FOUNDATION OF A RESILIENT GUJARAT

The decade that began in 2001 saw historical developments not just in Indian but the global context in improving cooperation and strengthening disaster preparedness and mitigation. The decade also witnessed some massive calamities. The Kutch earthquake shocked many with its magnitude and the scale of destruction. The tsunami that occurred in 2004 in the Indian Ocean was deadlier and claimed victims in over a dozen countries.

In 1999, Odisha was already devastated by a massive super cyclone. A few years later, there was a deadly earthquake in Kashmir, floods in Maharashtra and Bihar and Cyclone Nisha in Tamil Nadu. There were several major disasters in other parts of the world as well. Haiti saw a devastating earthquake in 2010, killing hundreds of thousands.

Consequently, governments across the world began working in greater coordination. With the 1990s being declared as the International Decade for Natural Disaster Reduction by the UN General Assembly, the research and awareness generated during this global initiative led to concrete effects in the succeeding decades.

The historic World Conference on Disaster Reduction was held in January 2005 in Kobe, Hyogo, Japan. The countries participating in the event adopted the Framework for Action 2005-2015: Building the Resilience of Nations and Communities to Disasters.[1]

This framework is often referred to as the Hyogo Framework. It identified five main areas for action and effective strategies to bring about the desired changes. These are as follows:[2]

Make disaster risk reduction a priority	Know the risks and take action	Build understanding and awareness	Reduce risk	Be prepared and ready to act

Disaster risk reduction became central to global efforts. It was widely understood that while disasters, natural or man-made, were inevitable, their effect could be minimized through the establishment of effective systems.

In India, Gujarat took the lead in enacting a comprehensive law providing a legal and regulatory framework for disaster management in 2003. Even as his government was working at a rapid pace to rebuild Kutch, Narendra Modi, as CM, guided his team to bring a comprehensive legislation in the field of disaster management. The state had come up with the GSDM policy in 2002 itself. The policy became a precursor to the Disaster Management Act, brought at the national level in 2005.[3] Gujarat was closely followed by Odisha. After the super cyclone of 1999 that killed thousands of people, Odisha had established its Disaster Management Authority headed by its CM.[4]

THE ROUTE TO DRR

Both Morbi in 1979, where Narendra Modi experienced the grim reality of a disaster-struck zone, and the Kutch earthquake in 2001, left a deep imprint on his mind. He realized that the state needed a more robust mechanism in dealing with disasters and their aftermath. The Morbi dam breach and the Kutch earthquake had both come without warning, catching the state unprepared. This was not acceptable. As CM, he was in a position to usher in the much-needed change. Chief Minister Narendra Modi began working to create a system under which Gujarat would be better informed about possible calamities and also better prepared. He focussed on an area that few political leaders in India have paid attention to—Disaster Preparedness.

As a state, Gujarat is particularly vulnerable to natural disasters. It is situated in the Himalayan Collision Zone, where the Indo-Australian tectonic plate tend to slide under the Eurasian plate with active fault lines underneath.[5] Gujarat also has a long coastline and is prone to cyclones.

Dr Manu Gupta, head of SEEDS (Sustainable Environment and Ecological Development Society), an NGO, recalls CM Modi's vision in supporting people's partnership across the disaster cycle of early warning, relief and rescue, thus contributing to a culture of preparedness.

A number of initiatives were taken in the state during this time that brought Gujarat to the forefront in the domain of DRR.

The Kutch earthquake had forced the state to review its mechanisms for disaster response and relief. A couple of weeks after the Kutch earthquake, on 8 February 2001, the Gujarat government created the GSDMA. The GSDMA was headed by the CM and had important cabinet ministers and top bureaucrats as its members.

'I recall the first meeting Chief Minister Narendra Modi attended as the chairman of the GSDMA. He promised that he would ensure that the authority becomes one of the best-administered disaster management programmes in the world,' recalls senior bureaucrat, Maheshwar Sahu.

The GSDMA definitely helped change the status quo. In 2003, the GSDMA received the UN Sasakawa Award for outstanding work in the field of disaster management.[6] Responsibilities of the GSDMA included coordination and monitoring of disaster prevention and mitigation activities, coordinating post-disaster reconstruction and rehabilitation, promoting awareness and preparedness, etc. The GSDMA in its initial years, drafted guidelines and policies for implementation in the state.[7] For instance, GSDM policy; guidelines for quality reconstruction and new construction of houses in earthquake-affected areas of Gujarat; guidelines for event management, etc.

In the long term, the GSDMA needed to be provided statutory foundations for DRR. It was during Narendra Modi's rule that Gujarat passed its Disaster Management Bill in March 2003.[8] Gujarat was the first state in India to introduce an Act of this kind.[9] The legislation came prior to the national disaster management law and, to an extent, served as a blueprint for it.

Disaster management frameworks of several countries were studied before the Gujarat government introduced the Act. There was a wide consultation with stakeholders. Apart from granting a statutory status to the GSDM Act, the Act envisages a multi-hazard approach to disaster management.

The legislation is based on the premise that disaster management is the responsibility of all the state departments and agencies. It lists in detail the powers, functions and duties of the departments and functionaries at state, district and sub-district levels.

The Act provides specific powers and responsibilities for the state government, the GSDMA, heads of government departments, relief commissioner, district collectors and local authorities. It involves community groups, youth organizations, industries, private and public sector entities, voluntary agencies and citizens. The Act also prescribes offences and penalties.

Subsequently, at the national level, the lessons learnt during the effective handling post-2001 Kutch earthquake, led to the enactment of the Disaster Management Act by the Union government on 23 December 2005.

The NDMA, which is the apex body of disaster management in India, was also established in 2005. The NDRF was formed on 19 January 2006. It currently consists of 16 battalions from the Border Security Force (BSF), Central Reserve Police Force (CRPF), Central Industrial Security Force (CISF), Indo-Tibetan Border Police (ITBP), Sashastra Seema Bal (SSB) and Assam Rifles. Formation of GSDMA further led to formation of various State Disaster Management Authorities (SDMAs).

Subjects like disaster management are often not prioritized by political parties, and the reason is rather simple. Disaster management is not considered to be a vote catcher. That is the reason that half a century had passed since independence, yet a coherent regulatory framework did not exist in any state or at the central level. Narendra Modi's aim was to create a state that had early warning mechanisms, preparedness and the capability to rehabilitate those affected. The state needed institutions that would be able to generate knowledge and nurture expertise in the field.

Vijay Rupani was CM Modi's colleague in the Gujarat Cabinet. He later also became the CM of the state. 'Kutch could be revived in a short period of time because of Narendra Modi's constant effort. More importantly, he emphasized on bringing disaster management as a separate department to the forefront,' says Rupani.

During the decade before the Kutch earthquake, there were earthquakes of high intensity that killed thousands in other parts of the world. These included the Kobe earthquake in Japan in 1995, Chi-Chi earthquake in Taiwan in 1999 and others.[10]

The Latur earthquake of 1993 in Maharashtra inflicted mind-numbing fatalities and destruction. Unfortunately, even after the Latur earthquake, India could not embark on the path of a resilient disaster preparedness model.

Kobe was a turning point in the disaster preparedness journey for Japan. For India, the Kutch earthquake was such a moment, primarily due to the proactive approach of the then Gujarat government under Narendra Modi.

After the Kutch earthquake, the government of Gujarat took the decision of not focussing only on speedy reconstruction but also creating a programme for disaster preparedness in the future. Institutions were built. Databases were created. Technology was put to optimum use, and innovation became the rule. A leaf or two were pulled out of the books of similar models from other parts of the world, like Japan.

According to senior bureaucrat P.K. Mishra, '[GSDMA] focused not only on the rehabilitation and reconstruction work but also on medium-term and long-term measures for disaster mitigation and preparedness. The creation of the GSDMA was the beginning of a new era. A new institutional structure emerged.'[11]

Speaking at an International Conference, 'Post Earthquake Reconstruction—Lessons Learnt and Way Forward', organized by the GSDMA in 2011, CM Modi said, 'The 2001 earthquake was a testimony to the power of nature and a test of resilience of people of Gujarat. The need of the hour was to achieve balanced and sustainable recovery in the earthquake-affected areas covering all aspects of human need. A need was also felt for a paradigm shift from the conventional approach of response post-disaster to mitigation and preparedness against disasters. [...] The first and foremost is creating of institutional mechanisms. The GSDMA was created as a permanent body not only to look at reconstruction, but also to undertake long-term disaster management in the state. All these institutional mechanisms were first of its kind in the reconstruction history of India. Gujarat reconstruction program become not only a successful program but also a model for many other reconstruction programs in India and Asia.'[12]

When the tsunami hit Tamil Nadu in 2004, Gujarat was a major state that gave support with valuable expertise in disaster relief and recovery efforts, including providing necessary models for reconstruction, based on its experience and research.

During Narendra Modi's tenure as Gujarat's CM, the state saw key institutions being created or strengthened capability-wise. Apart from the GSDMA, among the key institutions that came up were: the GIDM and Institute of Seismological Research (ISR).

As CM, Narendra Modi was of the clear view that preparations have always to be made in advance. Prevention is always more important than cure. To tackle a crisis situation, action had to be taken in a coordinated way with different government bodies. Therefore, systems had to be put in place first.

The GSDMA is entrusted with the responsibility of effectively managing disasters, mitigating their effects and providing emergency relief during disasters. However, it needs the support of bodies that could become repositories of expertise.

Naturally, when Narendra Modi was working in this domain, he was not only reimagining a regulatory-administrative framework for Gujarat but also providing a vision for similar efforts in the rest of the country at state as well as the central levels.

KEY TAKEAWAY

A paradigm shift from handling a disaster in a conventional manner to long-term disaster mitigation model is imperative. They should be reinforced by robust institutional frameworks that layout a roadmap towards preparedness.

BUILDING A ROBUST RESPONSE SYSTEM

Leaders who are able to build and nurture institutions and processes are invariably those who leave a long-lasting legacy. Narendra Modi shone as Gujarat's CM and one of the reasons for his success was his ability to build a system, marked with institutions and processes.

Having inherited a state that faced a huge gap in expertise and ability in disaster management, CM Modi wanted to create a mechanism that would stay abreast with the latest practices in the field of disaster management. He wanted institutions that would not only be a custodian of expert knowledge but also the training ground for officers and other stakeholders.

The GSDMA, under the CM, decided to develop a full-fledged institute for disaster management. A decision was taken on 12 March 2002 by the governing body to create the GIDM. In an enhanced role, it began working under the GSDMA. In 2012, it was registered as an 'autonomous body'. The Gujarat government then allotted land for the institute at Raisan near Gandhinagar. In August of the same year, the GIDM began functioning from its own campus.

Former IAS officer P. K. Taneja, who heads the GIDM, recalls that CM's focus was clear. The GIDM was to incorporate the best of research and technology. It had to actively disseminate its knowledge to officers, organizations and people across the state.

'In one of the meetings of the GIDM governing council, CM Modi made specific observations. He said the GIDM should prepare technology-based online training programmes on a large scale and make them accessible to people of the state. He asserted that the GIDM should aim to be the best institution in the world in the field of Disaster Management Training,' says Taneja.

Today, the GIDM functions as the apex institute in the state for disaster management capacity building, offering training related to disaster management, conducting community awareness activities and serving as a resource centre for disaster management information based on research and coordination with international bodies. It also provides dedicated courses on disaster management.

The earthquake that shook Kutch in January 2001 was one of the deadliest earthquakes to ever strike the region. Measuring 6.9 on the Richter scale, its intensity was exceptional. Kutch as a region was hardly a stranger to such tremors. The region experiences very high seismic activity. As CM, Narendra Modi was aware of this fact. He recognized an acute need of scientifically monitoring these movements. The 2001 earthquake caught Kutch completely off guard.

Was there a way to obtain accurate information and relay it to the appropriate agencies in a timely manner? CM and the top functionaries of his administration brainstormed to determine the best course of action. Consequently, Gujarat decided to set up its own ISR. The ISR is one of a kind institute fully dedicated to earthquake studies. It has a network of over 60 seismic stations and measures tremors round-the-clock. A majority of its seismic stations are located in the sensitive region of Kutch.[13] If information related to the occurrence of an earthquake took a couple of hours to reach the state government in the past, the ISR ensured it now arrived within a couple of minutes. The information is immediately shared with state and central disaster management authorities.

Under Narendra Modi's leadership, Gujarat made rapid progress towards becoming an advanced knowledge and industrial economy. The expertise of institutions like the ISR helped in making prime industrial installations from nuclear power plants, ports, to facilities like the petrochemical complex at Mundra or the Gujarat International Finance Tec (GIFT) city safer.

The ISR now regularly conducts studies related to the densely-populated areas of the state, including important towns like Jamnagar and Surat to suggest suitable norms. The central government also seeks the help and expertise of ISR with regard to planning for densely-populated towns in other states as well.

However, Narendra Modi's efforts to make Gujarat strong and resilient did not stay confined to just the trio of the GSDMA, GIDM and ISR. Gujarat also set up an International Institute of Chemical Safety and Research (IICSR). The institute was aimed to become an apex institute in the state for management of hazardous chemicals and play a crucial role in avoiding chemical disasters.

India had witnessed the horrific Bhopal gas tragedy in 1984 in the state of Madhya Pradesh where over 5 lakh people were exposed to toxic fumes emanating from the premises of a factory of the Union Carbide India Limited. It is considered as one of the worst industrial disasters in the world.[14]

Yet, expertise as well as awareness about these aspects remained limited even in the governing circles for decades. To bridge the gap, the IICSR was developed to focus on research and dissemination of information to create safer industrial zones. Additionally, a comprehensive Chemical and Industrial Disaster Management Plan for the State[15] and an Action Plan for Nuclear and Radiological Emergency were also developed.[16]

During his experiences as a volunteer, young Modi had witnessed the limitations of local authorities in dealing with emergency situations. For instance, an advance warning about the ominous rise of water levels on the Machhu River dam could have saved countless lives.

Governments often focus on the 5R approach to disaster management—Rescue, Relief, Restoration, Rehabilitation and Rebuilding. Narendra Modi augmented this approach by adding another 'R', which stands for 'Readiness'. His government worked to set up a system aligned to this foremost aspect. Time is of the essence in disaster response. A timely response can save countless lives. And that was the kind of approach that he exhibited right at the top.

Former GSDMA CEO V. Thiruppugazh witnessed how the CM paid attention even to the minutest bits of information. 'I worked in the GSDMA for several years. Many disasters have occurred during the night. So obviously, one of us had to inform the CM. I used to wake him up. At 12 o'clock in the night, sometimes at 3:00 in the morning. He would remain awake and available the whole night monitoring the situation,' says Thiruppugazh.

Former senior bureaucrat A.K. Sharma says that be it a road accident or fire incident, CM Modi knew it before them.

'Ninety per cent of the time, it was he who called us and shared the details. Chief Minister Narendra Modi had developed his own information-gathering mechanism in Gujarat through connect with the people,' says Sharma.

He did not want any section of the administration to hesitate in sharing information. It would only be through the exchange of information that an effective disaster management strategy could evolve.

If the establishment of global standard institutions was one part of the strategy, then creating a technology-driven information system was the next part. Gujarat, under Narendra Modi, became a pioneer not only in areas like disaster management but also in several other sectors. One of these was e-governance. Soon after Narendra Modi took charge as the CM, an area he gave immense impetus was exploring the possibility of information and communication technology (ICT).

In 2001–02, Gujarat rolled out one of the Asia's largest Government networks called the Gujarat State Wide Area Network (GSWAN), an IP-based network for communicating voice, data and video.[17] This became the backbone of disaster communication infrastructure. Later, for the first time in Asia, Gujarat upgraded the connectivity of all its local governing bodies, nearly 14,000 panchayats, through broadband.[18] The programme, launched in 2006 and called eGram Vishwagram, was a pioneering one in India.[19] The State Disaster Resource Network (SDRN), a web-based resource database, gathered and collated information regarding the availability of human resources, equipment and other necessary details.[20] Gujarat also became the pioneer state to implement the Incident Command System (ICS) in 2005.[21] A warning system called Disaster Alert and Resource Management by Application of Technology (DARMAT) was introduced as well.[22]

During the Surat floods in 2006, the handling of the disaster, including rescue, relief and rehabilitation, was speedily done so that the industrial city come back to normalcy within 72 hours. In fact, Surat floods turned out to be the first opportunity to test the efficacy of Gujarat's newly introduced disaster preparedness model, after the Kutch earthquake.

During the Surat floods, timely warning messages were sent to citizens, through SMS, FM radio and other means, which helped prevent a large number of fatalities. The database was of immense help then. At the national level, today, an India Disaster Resource Network (IDRN) is in place for the same purpose.

One of the key tasks that the GSDMA undertook under CM Modi was to carry out a mapping of the vulnerability. It created a detailed Hazard Risk and Vulnerability Atlas (HRVA) for Gujarat.[23] Major areas covered included earthquake, tsunami, flood, cyclone, drought and chemical and industrial hazards. The atlas was compiled on the basis of one of the most exhaustive databases created for hazard risk identification and advance planning. To create this database, all the talukas of Gujarat were surveyed. Gujarat is the pioneer state in extensively using GIS and remote sensing technology for this. Based on this detailed map, the GSDMA guided its major cities to change their building by-laws in a scientific manner to ensure safer construction of buildings.

STRENGTHENING CAPACITY

Former bureaucrat Maheshwar Sahu says that from 2001, the state government began working to make Gujarat one of the lowest-risk investment destinations in the country in terms of disaster. To achieve that, a primary task was capacity building, especially at lower levels. Strengthening the capacity of the state in dealing with emergency situations, especially at the levels of municipal bodies and panchayats, was a major challenge. The GSDMA focussed on this crucial task. Advanced equipment was procured and provided to grassroots. Firefighting services were upgraded with the latest equipment. Municipalities and corporations were equipped with fire tenders, water bowsers, motorcycle-powered mounted water mist systems, boats, state-of-the-art rescue vehicles, communication devices, etc. Command vehicles, urban search-and-rescue containers, medical casualty containers, high-capacity pumps and multifunctional rescue vehicles are also made available to Gujarat authorities in sufficient numbers.

A State Emergency Operation Centre (SEOC) was established to serve as the central command and control facility for emergency preparedness and disaster management. The aim was to ensure swifter mechanism for disaster warning and effective response. On the same lines, several District Emergency Operation Centres (DEOC) were also created. In addition, Regional Emergency Response Centres (ERCs) were set up at strategic locations—Rajkot, Vadodara, Surat, Gandhidham and Gandhinagar.

Gujarat also constructed several multi-purpose cyclone shelters. Many of these shelter homes were used during cyclone Tauktae in 2021. In the recent Biparjoy cyclone of 2023, nearly 1 lakh people from about eight districts were shifted to these multi-purpose cyclone shelters. Government buildings, schools and other buildings were also identified to serve as shelters at the time of disaster.[24]

Under the GSDM Act, the power to respond to the calamities were given to the district collectors and local authorities. The Act states that each department of the Government in a district shall prepare a disaster management plan for the district and the collector shall ensure that such plans are integrated into the disaster management plan for the entire district.

CM Modi wanted the plans to be decentralized. Hence, a model district-level plan was made for Jamnagar district. Later, this plan was sent to all the districts, instructing the district authorities to prepare their own plans. Thus, District Disaster Management Plans (DDMP) were drawn up. Gujarat today has disaster management plans at taluka, city and village levels.

'CM's focus was clear. The local authorities at the district and taluka levels are the first responders. Their capacity to deal with emergency situations had to be built. Second, awareness and knowledge had to transcend the official domain. Like in every activity he has undertaken, these efforts too were centred around local communities,' says G.R. Aloria, former Gujarat chief secretary.

However, it was necessary to ensure that district and local-level authorities were ready and trained to act professionally in case of any emergency. The GSDMA developed a range of learning materials and resources to train the system about disaster management and preparedness. Aspects related to disaster management were also taught in schools.

Gujarat aimed at preparing both the people and the administration to tackle emergency situations. Capacity building activities like orientation programmes, training, practical demonstration and awareness generation were conducted at all levels—village, taluka, city, municipal corporation and district. Mock drills and exercises began to be held regularly.

Narendra Modi recognized the strength of collective efforts. Village-, taluka- and district-level officials; organizations like Nehru Yuva Kendra (NYKS); National Service Scheme (NSS); NGOs; volunteers; skilled workers; doctors; corporates; schools and others were included in the comprehensive capacity-building plan.

'Following the Kutch earthquake of 2001, in our training in schools for students and teachers to build disaster preparedness for safety and security, CM Modi reminded us about how schools can be the building blocks for a society that is prepared to face disasters,' says Dr Manu Gupta.

'When the suggestion was made that the education department should come up with its own program for training students, the chief minister immediately approved. The program was rolled out for 55,000 schools across Gujarat. This idea that started with a few schools in Gujarat was eventually adopted at the national level,' says Gupta.

The GSDMA also began observing School Safety Week in educational institutions. Teachers and students were involved and sensitized about the various aspects of disaster management. CM Modi encouraged a community-based approach in every aspect. 'Gujarat started training disaster volunteers—Aapda Mitras. Community volunteers were trained for rescue operations and to assist the administration. Now the NDMA has made it a full-fledged national level program,' says former bureaucrat V. Thiruppugazh.

KEY TAKEAWAY

Capacity building for improved disaster preparedness should be an ongoing and all-encompassing effort. This involves not only training and preparing those at the macro level but also those at the micro level. In addition to the continuous upgrading of technology and equipment, human resource capacity building, which includes volunteers, should be a top priority.

TEST OF THE SYSTEM: 2006 SURAT FLOODS

As Chief Minister Narendra Modi worked to develop Gujarat's state apparatus, a challenge appeared in the state's southern commercial hub of Surat in 2006.

The city is located close to the point where Tapi River meets the Arabian Sea. In August 2006, after a rather harsh summer, Surat and its adjacent areas received plentiful rainfall. The pouring waters were, however, ominously raising the water level at the Ukai Dam complex. The Ukai Dam on the Tapi River is Gujarat's second-largest water reservoir. The dam is located at a distance of 94 km from Surat. The dam was constructed in 1972.[25] One of its objectives was to help manage floods that Surat experienced decade after decade. However, due to incessant rainfall, the dam's capacity proved inadequate.[26]

Like any other calamity, the Surat floods also resulted in significant economic losses, with estimates indicating damages exceeding ₹20,000 crore.[27] This was the biggest flood in nearly three-and-a-half decades in Gujarat. According to records, a much bigger flood had occurred in 1968.

As a volunteer, the altruistic Modi would rush to calamity-hit spots and participate in relief and rescue efforts. As Gujarat's CM, Narendra Modi was no different. Within hours, he was seen in the disaster-affected areas of Surat, leading the disaster management efforts from the front.

Pictures of Chief Minister Narendra Modi seated in an inflated boat examining the situation of the inundated town are widely available. That the CM himself reached the affected area and was supervising the relief efforts had a huge effect on the administrative machinery.

However, the Surat floods are important for another reason. This was one of the first major calamities that tested the efficacy of the GSDMA and the Disaster Management Plan that was born after the Kutch earthquake. The GSDMA, which was still in its early years, initiated efforts to ensure smooth coordination between various government departments.

The Gujarat government responded quickly. As soon as the information was brought to his notice, CM Modi instructed the concerned secretaries to put the entire machinery in motion. Evacuation efforts were initiated while arrangements for food packets and packaged drinking water were made. CM asked the local officials, including the collector, to provide him hourly updates.

The chief minister, along with other officials, immediately headed to the city with which he shares a strong emotional bond. On many occasions, political leaders assess the damage inflicted by calamities through aerial surveys aboard helicopters. Not only does it help them formulate an appropriate response strategy, but it also conveys a message to the people that the administration is doing its best for them. However, during the 2006 floods in Surat, the CM did not just tour the city but set up a base in the town and brought his top ministers and best officials to commence working.

Pravin Nanavati, a former president of Southern Gujarat Chamber of Commerce and Industry (SGCCI), recalls that 2006 marked one of the biggest floods that the city had seen. The massive inundation was just one part of the problem. There were many other hard challenges accompanying the deluge. Lakhs of people were affected, and they did not have access to food. There was water everywhere but it was not potable. The grain that people had stored became inedible.

However, Narendra Modi's presence provided Nanavati and other people of the city with immense hope. 'He set his camp in a school and from there assigned all ministers a particular area to ensure it was cleaned. CM Modi himself participated in the cleaning efforts,' says Nanavati. The CM actively ventured into the field, personally overseeing the progress of the work.

In addition to the government machinery, CM encouraged all social organizations to participate in the relief work. He instructed his officers that if they consider anything even of mild importance, they should call him, even in the middle of the night.

During the Surat floods, the technological roadmap for effective risk assessment and disaster prediction was still taking shape. But still, the authorities acted swiftly in alerting the people about a possible disaster. A warning about the rising waters in the dam was heard on 7 August. The administration tried to inform the people about the impending threat through vans deployed to disseminate information. Thousands of SMSs were sent to as many people as possible. Information was also released to the media.

Often, the poorer sections lack the means to relocate quickly. The administration began making efforts to remove as many people as possible from the city. Meanwhile, gushing waters began moving towards habitation. The low-lying areas were quickly submerged. The waters continued to rush in, and it was not until 11 August that the flow began to wane. The pace and magnitude of the inundation was such that an estimated 90 per cent of households were affected. Some areas reportedly had water levels as high as 90 feet. The government could evacuate thousands, preventing the possibility of huge loss of lives.

After a couple of days, as the waters began to recede, the next big challenge arose. Mud and sludge covered the town. CM Modi led the efforts to clean the city at a rapid pace. Volunteers and social organizations joined in. Cleaning Surat became a mission.

He took night walks in the muddy areas along with the officials, covering approximately 2–3 km. During these walks, he engaged in discussions regarding the necessary actions and strategies to be implemented. Locals recall that CM Modi went even at 1:00 a.m. to meet cleaners who were working round-the-clock.

After the floods, the first crucial step was to focus on cleaning homes and restoring cleanliness in the city. However, for this task, a continuous supply of water was necessary, which required the restoration of electricity to power the water supply systems.

In this endeavour, the experience gained from managing Morbi and Kutch disaster proved useful. The team that had dealt with the Kutch disaster management, known for their expertise in handling such situations, came forward to lend their assistance.

Former minister Saurabh Patel was in charge of the energy department. 'The entire city was submerged in water, including streets, main roads, societies and houses. It was impossible to provide electricity to households and societies. We planned a strategy to address this issue within 36–48 hours,' says Patel.

Efforts were made to procure electricity from various sources, and a team of engineers and workers was readied. 'Staff from all over Gujarat came with specific plans and they worked tirelessly. To everyone's surprise, electricity was restored within 24 to 36 hours in Surat,' adds Patel.

Nanavati remembers that the city began undergoing a transformation. 'CM Modi had cleaned the dirt off the road by himself and loaded it in a truck. This inspired the people to participate. Within 15 days, Surat was cleaned of the dirt that arrived due to the flood. The festival of Navratri was approaching, so he wanted normal life restored quickly,' says Nanavati.

Narendra Modi had pushed the entire government machinery at his disposal into flood relief work. Many locals recall that ministers who were outside Gujarat were asked to immediately rush back to the state. The stern-yet-committed attitude of the CM left no one in doubt that he wanted the relief and rehabilitation work in Surat to be carried out at a record pace and with unprecedented efficiency.

Many others recall the impact of Narendra Modi's stay in Surat during that most trying of times. Bharat Gandhi, an old associate of CM from Surat, recollects that the situation was such that it seemed it would take five years to rebuild the town. 'Within four days, Narendra Modi made sure most areas were clean. The power department worked with pace to restore electricity. Surat recovered just in three months,' he says.

'During his four to five-day stay in Surat, CM Modi attended to the smallest details, ensuring that children had access to milk, providing food for the less fortunate and actively participating in rescue operations for those stranded by the floodwaters,' says Purnesh Modi, an MLA from Surat.

As a leader, Narendra Modi likes to be hands-on. However, he is also quick to acknowledge people with special capabilities and delegate responsibility. During the Surat floods, he utilized the acumen and ability of a former commissioner who had done outstanding work in the area.

Locals recall how CM Modi brought in one of his best officials, S.R. Rao, to supervise the relief and rehabilitation work. Not only that, he also delegated authority to the officer to ensure the task was accomplished efficiently. Rao had worked in Surat earlier as Municipal Commissioner and knew the town and its people well. 'Rao served as the commissioner of Surat. Such was his work that he was widely respected in the city. CM Modi sent him to Surat to lead the mission. Later, we came to know that he gave him the authority to act on his behalf and report directly to him. The aim was to ensure fast-paced relief and rehabilitation,' says Nanavati.

Along with Rao, senior minister I.K. Jadeja was also stationed in Surat by CM Modi to oversee the work. Bureaucrat M.S. Patel was another key officer who worked in the team. Patel recalls that it was known to them that CM was especially fond of Surat and its people. He says that detailed plans would be drawn up for every task that was undertaken.

Work began in earnest, and then came information that the CM would soon arrive in Surat. The officials were in a quandary. The circumstances of the city were quite inhospitable.

'We were worried. No car or jeep could move on the road in the city. There was so much water. Then S.R. Rao had an idea. He called a fire engine, and the three of us went to receive CM Modi when his helicopter landed,' says Patel.

He immediately entered the cabin of the fire engine and said that he would like to immediately assess the situation in the worst-affected part of the town. Without delay, CM, along with his team of officials, reached Chowk Bazar.

Patel recalls that as they passed through the inundated localities, people who had climbed to the top of three or four-storey buildings, started showing empty utensils to the CM. They also conveyed that there was no water to drink. 'There was no water supply because of the flood. There was water everywhere, including the control room and even the collector's office, but no drinking water,' says Patel.

With the help of the CRPF, the control room was shifted to a school. 'We converted the teachers' room into a control room,' says Patel. It was in this control room that CM Modi met top officials.

Patel has a vivid memory of one such meeting, in which several top Gujarat officials were present. The discussion on how to remedy the situation had just begun when a peon brought glasses of water in a tray. Refusing to take even a sip, CM announced '*Surat ki janta jab tak paani nahi piyegi tab tak main bhi paani nahi piyunga*' (Till the time people of Surat do not have water to drink, I will also not take even a sip of water).

The atmosphere in the meeting became even more serious. The CM had made known the level of his anguish. Patel says, 'The effect it had on the system was such that the work, which had to be completed in 48 hours was accomplished in 24. [...] The state government officials had earlier estimated that it would take them 48 hours to restore water supply. The tanks were filled with mud-water, and there was no power supply. We quickly completed all the work so that not only the people of Surat but also the CM could drink water.'

CM Modi did not only ensure that the water was available to everyone; he asked officials to ensure that its quality was healthy. Contaminated water can lead to spread of diseases, which can complicate rehabilitation efforts.

'During the flood in Surat, the civil hospital itself was inundated, posing additional challenges. Within 48 hours of the flood receding, the government swiftly provided all necessary requirements for both the people and the hospital. One major concern during this time was a potential outbreak of gastroenteritis due to the lack of clean water. Recognizing this threat, CM Modi made a crucial decision to create a detailed plan to ensure a safe water supply,' says Dr Nimesh Varma, who worked in the city at that time.

The availability of medicines, doctors, hospitals and other experts is crucial during times of crisis. Recognizing this need, the practice of maintaining a list of experts was initiated by the authorities. This proactive approach proved to be beneficial in coordinating rescue and relief efforts effectively. Through rosters of skilled professionals, including doctors, healthcare workers, engineers and other relevant experts, disaster response efforts can be expedited and optimized.

KEY TAKEAWAY

Political will is crucial in challenging times. However, in situations where speed is of the essence, decisions should be made by individuals with the expertise and maturity required for handling crises. Making the wrong decision can have devastating consequences.

Narendra Modi had rushed to Morbi, Kutch and other sites as a volunteer. He always stressed on collective effort and community participation as fundamental aspects of disaster management. Those who saw him working as CM could sense the same streak in his actions as he worked in Surat. Here was a CM not afraid to enter muddy waters. He was willing to take up a broom and clean the area. This attitude inspired not just the administrative machinery but the local people as well. Surat belonged to all of them, and they were going to restore it together.

As a result of this collective endeavour, the city was largely cleaned up within a remarkable span of 15 days. Hundreds of volunteers participated in the cleaning and other relief activities. Surat later started the practice of compiling details of such resources on the SDRN database.

Narendra Modi's concept of converting disaster into an opportunity was also at play in Surat. He asked the municipal bodies in Surat and the Gujarat government to take a number of steps to rebuild the city. For instance, the Surat Municipal Corporation utilized funds from the Jawaharlal Nehru National Urban Renewal Mission (JNNURM) to augment the city's stormwater drainage network and sewerage network.

The Surat floods helped in developing local plans. Surat developed its own disaster management plan, which not only helped in managing the situation during floods but also charted long-term measures to avoid similar disasters in the city and equip it better.

The GSDMA and other agencies, based on their research and experience of Surat floods, could come up with better risk assessment studies. A contour survey was done based on the flood map of Surat in 2006, which helped in preparing a flood prediction map for the city. The Surat experience was also utilized in building the SEOC that came into existence in 2010.

CM Modi's efforts and the newly developed disaster management system under the GSDMA brought quick relief and helped in bringing normalcy to the deluge-hit town. More importantly, Surat also helped improve the new paradigm of disaster management that Gujarat had adopted.

India is a rumbunctious democracy, and like any other event, the Surat floods were also the subject of political confrontation.

To address all concerns and look for lessons to be learned, CM Modi's government appointed a commission to examine the entire incident. In 2008, Justice Sugnaben Bhatt Commission's report was presented in the state assembly. The commission found that the administration had taken appropriate steps in dealing with the situation.[28]

Many people also tried to chronicle the work done in Surat by Chief Minister Narendra Modi, Rao and the other members of the team. Dinkar Naik and others at the Seva Setu Trust also decided to publish a book for future reference. 'So we published a book titled *Mahre Surat 2006*,' says Naik. The group was pleasantly surprised when the chief minister, despite his busy schedule, decided to attend its launch. On the day of the event, it was his advice that Naik and others found very valuable.

'Why don't you create a website for it? Make a website for it and develop a disaster management structure so that whenever a natural calamity hits us, ensure that you have backup for that. List all the voluntary organizations in your city who are ready to do useful work in such a scenario,' CM Modi told Naik and others. Naik says that not only did the then CM boost their efforts, but he also gave them a pathway to move forward.

Gujarat later witnessed several other small and large disasters, including various cyclones like Tauktae, Vayu and Biparjoy as well as floods like that of 2017. During the 2017 floods, the government could evacuate more than 1 lakh people. By then, Gujarat was ready to tackle the disasters better, saving thousands of lives and recovering fast.

Preparedness and mitigation were the twin mantras of the Gujarat disaster management model under Narendra Modi. Instead of the conventional reactive approach, it tried to take a proactive route. In a few years, Gujarat moved to become the pioneer state when it came to establishing a mechanism for emergency response.

The state came to occupy a position where it could swiftly come to the aid of other Indian states when it came to disaster response. Subsequently, at the national level, most of the best practices of Gujarat helped the NDMA to prepare India better for disasters.

Chapter 5

The Making of a Resilient Nation

CAPACITY BUILDING AT NATIONAL LEVEL

In 2014, strong winds of political change blew across India. The people, especially the younger generation, were tired of the prevailing status quo and sought change in the way the country was governed.

Narendra Modi, who was then the CM of Gujarat, stood for that change. The Gujarat model became an oft-repeated phrase ahead of the elections. The western state, under him excelled in various parameters, positioning him in a unique space. Having governed Gujarat for nearly 13 years, for many, Narendra Modi became the obvious choice as India's next PM.

One reason was that his proactive approach often became visible outside his home state. The Uttarakhand floods of 2013 was one such occasion. On 17 June 2013, torrential rains of an unprecedented magnitude fell on the Himalayan hill state. Despite being the CM of another state, Narendra Modi not only provided financial and material assistance but also reached the affected areas. The matter also became a subject of controversy as his efforts evoked comparisons with those of the UPA (United Progressive Alliance) government that ruled at the centre at that time. However, it also brought the subject of disaster management into focus and raised pertinent questions about the preparedness of the system.

Then CM of Uttarakhand, Vijay Bahuguna, says that during the 2013 floods, he received calls from several CMs of the country and many had sent help. 'Narendra Modi visited personally. He not only handed over a cheque from Gujarat government but also brought with him a group of officers and experts who had huge experience in disaster relief, especially the Kutch earthquake. Their expertise helped our team handle the disaster in a better way. He sought the responsibility of rebuilding the Kedarnath Dham on a grand scale. I was immensely influenced by his understanding of disaster management and his concern for people in distress,' says Bahuguna. PM Modi fulfilled his resolve to restore Kedarnath and its surrounding areas by 2017.

This hands-on approach held Narendra Modi in good stead during the 2014 general elections when his party won a historic mandate. The victory, however, brought with it important responsibilities. Many areas were going to see changes, and one of the fields that saw a comprehensive debate and significant augmentation was DRR.

The mandate proved to be a historical one even from the disaster response readiness perspective. Interestingly, Narendra Modi made his priority clear from the beginning. He decided to involve the people in his efforts to build a more resilient country.

DISASTER MANAGEMENT APPARATUS IN INDIA TILL 2014

As mentioned earlier, even after five decades of Independence, India did not have a comprehensive legal mechanism to deal with calamitous situations.

Gujarat became the first state to enact a comprehensive law in 2003, following which the central government also brought the Disaster Management Act in 2005.[1] A three-tier system that envisaged cooperation between the centre, the states and local authorities was envisaged and created. The NDMA was set up along with the state disaster management authorities.

However, the implementation of any law is needed on the ground. Its presence on paper is just the first step towards the desirable outcomes. Naturally, when the Comptroller and Auditor General (CAG) brought out a vital report in 2013 on the status of disaster management in India, glaring lacunae and gaps emerged.[2] The institutions set up under the disaster management laws were still in their infancy. The system existed on paper yet needed to be bolstered on ground. 'We found that despite considerable progress in setting up institutions and creating funding arrangements, there are critical gaps for the preparedness levels of various disasters,' the CAG said in its report tabled in Parliament in 2013.

Among the gaps that the CAG pointed out, there were many fundamental operational aspects. According to the report, the National Executive Committee of Secretaries to assist the NDMA had not met for several years after May 2008. The country has faced many disasters since, it said. A national plan for disaster management had not been formulated even six years after the enactment of the of Disaster Management Act the audit mentioned.

The audit felt that there was much improvement needed in the functioning of the NDMA. It had glaring vacancies. The National Database for Emergency Management (NDEM), scheduled for completion by August 2011, had not been put into operation. The effectiveness of the NDRF was hampered due to a shortage of trained manpower, facilities and equipment.

These are just a few of the areas in which the comprehensive CAG report found gaps. It found that the steps taken to address challenges such as chemical disasters, nuclear threats, epidemics, forest fires and others were not adequate.

P.K. Mishra, who was the CEO of the GSDMA earlier, was appointed to head a task force by the Union home ministry in 2012–13 to review the Diasater Management Act of 2005. The taskforce suggested empowering the NDMA and giving authority to prepare a national plan for Disaster Management.[3] It also pointed out that the NDMA members should have expertise in disaster management rather than being political appointees, as was the practice during the UPA government.

The NDMA was almost in a state of dysfunction. There was a lack of synergy among various stakeholders like NDMA, NDRF, states and also the National Crisis Management Committee (NCMC), which the taskforce pointed out.

While some progress had been made since 2001, there was still much work ahead to enhance the nation's preparedness. Disaster response is inherently challenging and requires ongoing effort. To address this, political leadership should prioritize disaster management as an essential area of focus.

TRANSFORMATION BEGINS

The ascent of Narendra Modi in the Indian political scene meant redefined national priorities. As the CM of Gujarat and even before that, he had worked extensively to provide succour to people when they faced disasters. Naturally, the domain of DRR received much attention after he took over as the fourteenth PM of India.

However, barely a couple of months into his new office, PM Modi had to supervise efforts in flood-hit Kashmir. Kashmir witnessed heavy rainfall in September 2014. Jhelum River was inundated, flooding hundreds of villages and the city of Srinagar. Nearly 300 lives were lost. Landslides followed and several bridges and roads were destroyed.[4]

PM Modi promptly visited the state for a first-hand assessment. The Jammu & Kashmir CM briefed PM Modi about the damage that had taken place. The prime minister's presence on the field and his proactive approach, like at the times of Morbi, Kutch and Surat, played an important role in speedy relief and recovery. Under his leadership, senior officials, including the home secretary, were stationed in the state, coordinating relief and recovery.

Tens of thousands of people were evacuated in record time by the army and other forces. Thousands of metric tonnes of food items were distributed, including ready-to-eat food items. Pumps from the oil wells of the Oil and Natural Gas Corporation (ONGC) and other mines were airlifted for pumping out water from Srinagar. Hundreds of medical teams were availed on the field. For filtering water, RO plants with vast capacity, were transported from other parts of the country to the state. Thousands of blankets were distributed.

The Jammu–Srinagar national highway, which was affected by floods and landslides, was reopened in record time, with the help of Border Roads Organisation (BRO). Power transmission lines were restored within days.

Prime Minister Narendra Modi noted that the allocated ₹1,100 crores to the state through the State Disaster Relief Fund would be insufficient given the scale of the tragedy. As a result, he took steps to secure an additional special project assistance of ₹1,000 crore from the Union government for flood relief and rehabilitation in the state.

Soon after the flood recovery activities, reconstruction of infrastructure, including roads, bridges and buildings, was rapidly undertaken. Thrust was placed on restoring the livelihoods of people.

The youth of Kashmir, often portrayed by dubious designs as being against Indian armed forces, were seen hugging them and showing their love and respect to the soldiers. Prime Minister Narendra Modi also offered support to people across the Line of Control (LoC) as well after learning of their plight.

Some of the main highlights of Kashmir flood mitigation exercise, as experts point out, are: the unprecedented coordination of stakeholders and resources, resulting in a speedy recovery; the leadership of PM Modi, who had more hands-on experience of disaster management than any other political leader in the country; and not limiting to basic recovery but ensuring a comprehensive return to normalcy, through infrastructure rebuilding and restoring livelihoods, instead of only basic recovery.

Kashmir floods happened a few months after Narendra Modi became the PM, but it also gave an early opportunity for the system to adopt the best practices of disaster management for which Gujarat had already set a template.

Barely a few days later, a cyclone hit parts of Andhra Pradesh and Odisha. PM Modi again got in touch with the state governments and offered assistance. The Indian Meteorological Department (IMD) had, on this instance, provided a timely warning.

Just as it was visible in Kashmir, Andhra Pradesh and Odisha, PM Modi espoused the spirit of Cooperative Federalism. In the wake of subsequent disasters across the nation, he consistently led from the forefront, embracing a democratic approach that included state leadership, local officials and the affected populace. His disaster management approach serves as a testament to his belief in the concept that disaster management is a collective effort.

He always tried to personally visit disaster-affected areas, along with the local administrative leadership. He undertook first-hand stock-taking surveys to assess the extent of damage and destruction. For instance, he did aerial surveys of the region affected by the Bihar Floods (2017), Kerala Floods (2018), and Cyclone Fani in Odisha (2019), amongst others. His interactions extended beyond meeting officials. He would try to meet victims; he would seek to uplift their spirits and morale, much like his earlier roles as an ordinary volunteer during the Morbi disaster in 1979 and the Kutch earthquake. Despite the attempts by some state governments to politicize his efforts, Narendra Modi's disaster management model focuses on inclusivity. He has reiterated time and again that both the Centre and States represent 'Team India' and must collaborate to foster development and progress.

In April 2015, a massive earthquake rocked Nepal. Again, PM Modi was quick to react and provided maximum assistance to the brother-like Himalayan nation. In a radio address on 26 April 2015, Narendra Modi expressed his sentiments regarding the destruction wreaked by calamities. 'I have seen Kutch earthquake very closely on 26 January 2001. I can clearly imagine how devastating these disasters are. I can imagine what Nepal and the victimised families there must be going through. But my dear brothers and sisters of Nepal, India is with you in your hour of grief. Work has begun to provide assistance to people facing crisis across several locations in India and Nepal,' he said in his radio address.

'First and foremost work is rescue operation to save people. Some people must still be alive under the debris and should get evacuated safely from there. A team of experts which has been sent is specifically trained for this task. Sniffer dogs have been sent as they possess the ability to trace any individual staying alive under the debris. Our whole endeavour would be to save maximum number of people alive. Post rescue operation, there is a need to undertake relief work as well. Rehabilitation work will also continue for long. India will make sure to wipe the tears of every Nepali, hold their hands and provide support to them,' PM Modi added.[5]

Member secretary of the NDMA, Kamal Kishore, attended a meeting where PM Modi discussed ways to help Nepal. 'Prime Minister Narendra Modi has had a personal experience in Bhuj reconstruction and recovery after the 2001 earthquake. So, when you talk to him, his experience reflects in his talk. For example, he gave the idea that people who have lost their homes will have to live under the open sky or in tents and so to protect them from cold, we should give them warm water bottles so that they can keep themselves warm,' says Kishore.

Prime Minister Narendra Modi also suggested that since Nepal will receive help from all across the world and its air traffic will be overwhelmed, India should see how it can help the former in managing logistics. Kishore says that India's help was the most substantial among all countries. 'It was our responsibility since it is our close neighbour and we share good relations with Nepal,' he says.

India's support to Nepal was not just limited to the aftermath of the calamity. 'Until 2021 we have worked in villages in Nepal. We have constructed more than 50,000 permanent houses there,' says Kishore.

In many of his widely-heard *Mann Ki Baat* addresses, PM Modi has repeatedly spoken about the subject of DRR. In his speech on 29 November 2015, PM Modi informed the people that after the Nepal earthquake, he had even mooted the idea that SAARC nations should come together for a joint exercise on disaster preparedness.[6]

NATIONAL DISASTER MANAGEMENT PLAN

As mentioned earlier, the comprehensive CAG audit on disaster preparedness had mentioned that years after the passing of the Disaster Management Act, there was no national disaster management plan in place. On 1 June 2016, this key task was fulfilled. Prime Minister Modi released the first-ever National Disaster Management Plan (NDMP) prepared in the country.[7]

The plan was based on the four priority themes of the 'Sendai Framework,' which focusses on four pillars—understanding disaster risk, improving disaster risk governance, investing in DRR and, above all, preparedness. The Sendai Framework for DRR (2015–30) succeeded the Hyogo Framework (2005–15) and was adopted at the World Conference on DRR in Sendai, Japan, in June 2015.[8]

The NDMA assigned roles and responsibilities at various levels of the government, from panchayat and urban local bodies to officials working in ministries at centre and state levels. It is scalable according to the requirements of the situation.

The plan was based on many of the approaches that PM Modi had implemented on ground in Kutch and other areas. Experts from a wide range of disciplines contributed to its formulation. The NDMP was further revised in 2019 to make it more comprehensive. The revised plan includes new hazards like thunderstorms, lightning, squalls, cloudbursts, etc. The CAG report had mentioned that several of these calamities were not part of the DRR strategies. It also includes Climate Change Risk Management as a new thematic area for risk-informed development. This NDMP delineated time-bound actions for all ministries departments to match the timelines of the global Sendai Framework for DRR.

Meanwhile, other areas that the CAG report mentioned were also being addressed. A National Disaster Mitigation Fund has also been set up in 2021 while work in other areas gathered pace. The National Fund was provided ₹13,000 crore while ₹32,000 crore was kept for State Disaster Mitigation Fund.[9]

PM MODI'S TEN SUTRAS ON DRR

Disasters and calamities do not consider national boundaries as an obstacle. The tsunami that struck in 2004 affected dozens of countries. Tremors of earthquake in Afghanistan have the potential to be felt in India, Pakistan and elsewhere. Therefore, a key aspect of PM Modi's outlook at the discipline has been that disasters are a human problem that should be faced by nations collectively.

In November 2016, under PM Modi's leadership, an important global conference on Disaster Risk Reduction was held in New Delhi. The Asian Ministerial Conference on Disaster Risk Reduction was the first such gathering after the adoption of the Sendai Framework. It was here that he gave one of the most influential speeches—a virtual framework on the subject.

PM Modi mentioned that over the last two decades, the world had seen many changes, most of them positive. 'Many countries in our region have transformed their economies and become engines of global economic growth. Hundreds of millions of our people have been lifted out of poverty. The Asia-Pacific region has been a global leader in more ways than one. [...] This progress cannot be taken for granted and there are challenges as well...Over the last twenty years, more than eight hundred and fifty thousand people died from disasters in the Asia-Pacific,' he said. [10]

'I have seen for myself the human suffering caused by disasters. I witnessed the Gujarat earthquake of 2001, and later, as Chief Minister of the State, I worked with my people to support post-earthquake recovery. It was distressing to see the suffering of the affected people. But I was also inspired by their courage, ingenuity and resolve to recover from the disaster. In my experience, the more we relied on people's own leadership, the better were the outcomes,' he mentioned.[11]

The prime minister specifically highlighted a core of his focus, community participation for disaster recovery. 'For example, when we entrusted the community the task of reconstructing a school, the earthquake-resistant building was completed in time, at a lesser cost, and the savings were returned to Government. We need to support such initiative and leadership through policies and practices,' he mentioned. [12]

He outlined at the conference a 10-point agenda for renewing global efforts towards DRR:[13]

1. All development sectors must imbibe the principles of disaster risk management
2. Risk coverage must include all, starting from poor households to SMEs to multi-national corporations to nation states
3. Women's leadership and greater involvement should be central to disaster risk management
4. Invest in risk mapping globally to improve global understanding of nature and disaster risks
5. Leverage technology to enhance the efficiency of disaster risk management efforts
6. Develop a network of universities to work on disaster-related issues
7. Utilise the opportunities provided by social media and mobile technologies for disaster risk reduction
8. Build on local capacity and initiative to enhance disaster risk reduction
9. Make use of every opportunity to learn from disasters and, to achieve that, there must be studies on the lessons after every disaster
10. Bring about greater cohesion in international response to disasters

The 10-point agenda by PM Modi now has laid the foundation for disaster management model not only for new India but also for the world, which was looking for answers since the 1990s when nations came together to evolve a disaster management model for the future. The most significant aspect of the 10-point agenda is that it is comprehensive and holistic. It covers many aspects that many nations and models have overlooked.

The 10-point agenda is so inclusive in every aspect, says Rajib Shaw, an expert of disaster management based out of Japan, who was also present at the conference. He worked earlier in the Kutch rebuilding programme. 'We got the opportunity to work on developing a university network in India, focusing on disaster management, as was mentioned in one of the 10 points. We, working along with the UN, the National Institute of Disaster Management (NIDM), the NDMA and several universities could create a network called the Indian University Network for Disaster Risk Reduction,' he states.

One of the key aspects that PM Modi consistently stressed, was one of his 10 principles—to extract valuable lessons from each disaster management experience and continuously enhance capabilities, says Atul Karwal, who holds the position of director general for India's specialized disaster response force, the NDRF. Recalling a recommendation from PM Modi, Karwal says, 'As Cyclone Jawad approached the eastern coasts of India in December 2021, PM Modi called a special meeting. During the discussion, he mentioned the importance of improving disaster management based on previous experiences and lessons learned. Subsequently, when Cyclone Biparjoy struck in 2023, not a single casualty occurred because we followed his recommendation to learn from the experience of Cyclone Jawad.'

'Following the Operation Dost mission by India in the 2023 Turkey earthquake, which included the NDRF, the army and other personnel, Prime Minister Narendra Modi hosted a reception at his residence for the contingent. During this gathering, he emphasized the importance of learning from every disaster as a lesson for the future. He enquired whether the team had observed the activities of teams from other nations during international missions, including the equipment they use, their protocols, training methods and more. He encouraged us to document international mission experiences, which can help enhance India's disaster response capabilities,' adds Karwal.

PM Modi's 10 guiding principles place a strong focus on DRR, with an emphasis on proactive approaches built on past experiences. The current priority is capacity building, as highlighted by Atul Karwal.

'*SABKA PRAYAS*' MODEL OF PREPAREDNESS

The Indian disaster response mechanism grew from a phase of calamities inflicted by negligence during foreign rule to a phase where disasters were still seen as acts of gods about which little could be done. The 1990s were a decade when global awareness about disaster response was generated. However, in India, the most substantial changes came post 2001, after the rude jolts of the Kutch earthquake.

While a legal mechanism, in the form of the Disaster Management Act had been put in place, and many important initiatives were carried out, much was needed to be done in terms of capacity building. The country was becoming more and more urbanized and this led to a different set of challenges. Given its burgeoning population, the scale of any event in India is huge. The rapidly increasing population, along with urbanization, created its own pressures and challenges.

However, post 2014, PM Modi's government invested heavily in new technologies, expertise and capacity building as well as ushered in a new culture of preparedness and resilience. By 2021, at least 33 states and Union Territories (UTs) had their approved state disaster management plans in place. This is a vital aspect as disaster management primarily comes under the domain of the respective state under the Disaster Management Act.

'Narendra Modi is the first person in the country to come up with a comprehensive State Disaster Management Act in Gujarat, back in 2003. Perhaps India is the only nation where a state or province enacted a law on Disaster Management before the centre did,' says Lieutenant General Syed Ata Hasnain, an Indian army veteran and member of the NDMA. A paradigm shift in disaster management was seen after 2014, especially focusing on the 10-point agenda of PM Modi, asserts General Hasnain.

However, PM Modi's focus throughout has been community-led resilience. As a volunteer, he has experienced community service and led a team of volunteers during Morbi floods in 1979. Later in Kutch, he converted the disaster management programme into a *Jan Andolan* (people's movement). When Gujarat was preparing its own model of disaster preparedness, he gave predominant priority to community participation, volunteerism and local capacity building.

'PM Modi has always said that Jan Bhagidari (People's Participation) is very important for disaster management and this is possible by giving the local community a stake in the work they do,' says Krishna Vatsa, member of the NDMA.

In the 10-point agenda as well, PM Modi emphasized it. 'Over the last two decades, most community-based efforts have been confined to disaster preparedness and contingency planning for the short term. We need to expand the scope of community-based efforts and support communities to identify local risk reduction measures and implement them. Such efforts reduce risk and create opportunities for local development and sustainable livelihoods. Localisation of DRR will also ensure that we make the most of traditional best practices and indigenous knowledge,' he appealed to the nation and world community in the 2016 Asian Ministerial Conference, highlighting the need to augment community participation in disaster management.[14]

PM Modi encouraged a unique scheme of training volunteers called Aapda Mitras, especially in 350 of the most vulnerable districts.[15] During the relief efforts for Cyclone Biparjoy in 2023, Aapda Mitras played a significant role.

'He gave us the initial target of training 1 lakh Aapda Mitras in every district of the country. Every village should have an Aapda Mitra. He suggested including local sports clubs, divers and other volunteers in the scheme,' says Kishore. Currently around 80,000 Aapda Mitras have been trained by the NDMA.

Disaster management has now turned out into a 'Sabka Prayas' model, says PM Modi.[16]

Kamal Kishore remembers that the PM gave an example to imagine how community participation can be ensured. 'He brought into our notice that forest fires generally occur due to pine needles that fall from pine trees. He suggested why they can be collected and recycled by the locals in the area and create products from them. It will generate livelihood and also curb forest fires.'

In March 2023, PM Modi addressed a meeting of the National Platform for Disaster Risk Reduction (NPDRR), which includes various union ministers, state government representatives, etc. He shared vital perspectives gained from years of tackling disaster situations to create a roadmap for the future. For instance, he referred to the importance of traditional knowledge. Citing the Kutch earthquake, the prime minister pointed out that the mud-dwellings of tribals, referred to locally as bhungas, remained intact while modern buildings collapsed. 'When we link the Future Technology with such examples of Local Resilience, only then we will be able to get better in the direction of disaster resilience,' said PM Modi.[17]

He raised the aspect of strengthening the capacities of Urban Local Bodies. 'It is not enough for the Urban Local Bodies to react only when a disaster strikes. We have to institutionalize the planning. We have to review the local planning. We need to make new guidelines for the construction of buildings and for new infrastructure projects keeping in mind the disaster management. In a way, overhauling of the entire system is needed,' he averred. It was in this speech that PM Modi gave the important mantra—'Local Resilience by Local Participation'.[18]

'When it comes to disaster management, that is not possible without public participation. You can achieve success only by following the mantra of "Local Resilience by Local Participation". It should be a continuous process to make citizens aware of the dangers associated with earthquakes, cyclones, fires and other disasters. It is necessary to continuously create awareness on all these subjects related to the right rules, regulations and duties,' he said.[19]

The power of Aapda Mitra, the NCC, the NSS and ex-servicemen should be utilized by creating a data bank and also making arrangements for swift communication, he suggested.

'While Cyclone Jawad was approaching, one of the valuable suggestions PM Modi provided was to meet with the members of Parliament representing the areas expected to be affected by the cyclone. Since the Parliament session was on, a meeting was arranged specifically for these parliamentarians, during which the NDRF and other experts briefed them on how to disseminate information to their constituents in their respective regions. This information included the necessary actions during a disaster, the cooperation required from the people for evacuation and other safety-related measures. PM Modi's approach ensures that disaster management is a collective effort, and all relevant stakeholders should be actively involved,' explains Atul Karwal.

Moreover, Karwal points out that during impending disasters, PM Modi leads from the front, conducting meetings with all relevant departments and stakeholders, leaving no room for coordination gaps.

During the reception held at the PM's residence for the rescue team dispatched to Turkey after the earthquake in 2023, PM Modi personally approached the team members and interacted with them. He was aware that there were five female rescuers in the team and even knew that one of them had left her young twin children at home to join the mission. He specifically sought her out and extended his personal appreciation. 'It was a heartwarming gesture that boosted the morale of the mission team,' says NDRF chief Karwal.

In the 10-point programme, PM Modi specifically laid emphasis on women. 'It is one area that most people tend to overlook in disasters. In any calamity, the people who suffer the most are women and children. PM Modi did not look at women as simply victims but also made suggestions to ensure women leadership in disaster management,' says General Hasnain. He also added that it is amply clear that PM Modi's vision of disaster management is not only comprehensive but also incorporates the smallest and even unseen aspects of it.

The Subhash Chandra Bose Aapda Prabandhan Puraskar was instituted to be conferred on individuals and organizations who contributed in the field of disaster management. Such an award is new to any country. It aims at promoting more people's participation in disaster management.

The fire station in Lunglei, Mizoram, received the award in 2023 for its exemplary response to a large forest fire that occurred in April 2021, covering the areas surrounding Lunglei town. The dedicated efforts of the Lunglei Fire Station personnel successfully contained the fire after working continuously for more than 32 hours.[20]

'During a meeting, PM Modi provided an example from Gujarat, highlighting a situation where the construction of a highway resulted in the obstruction of the natural water flow. Consequently, during the monsoon season, the highway remained unaffected while the villages on the sides of the highway were subjected to flooding. In light of this, PM Modi recommended that India's infrastructure development should not only be resilient to disasters but should also ensure that it does not create downstream risks', recalls Kamal Kishore. The PM also highlighted the aspect that India's disaster management model should not only focus on saving lives but also saving infrastructure, as the economic stress caused by disasters is equally painful.

India's disaster management now focuses not only on a few areas but on a wide range of possible disasters. Lightning, heatwaves, forest fires, coastal erosion—no stone is left unturned. 'He held a meeting in the winter of Delhi, in February, to discuss preparations for a heatwave in the upcoming summers,' recalls Krishna Vatsa.

Prime Minister Narendra Modi was not only working towards building a more robust and resilient India but was also willing to share his experience from Morbi to Kutch and beyond with the world. He consistently promoted a vision in which countries would stand as partners in addressing disasters, aligning with India's ethos of 'Vasudaiva Kutumbakam'.

In 2019, PM Modi took this idea one step further when he launched the Coalition for Disaster Resilient Infrastructure

(CDRI). It involves 34 countries—America, Australia, Japan, the Maldives, Mongolia, Dominican Republic, France, Germany, Italy and many more developed and developing nations.[21]

On 28 August 2019, the Union Cabinet of India headed by PM Modi took another important step as it approved the setting up of the CDRI with its Secretariat in New Delhi along with a support of ₹480 crore. The support from Government of India (GoI) serves as a corpus for the CDRI to fund technical assistance and research projects on an ongoing basis, setting up the Secretariat office and covering recurring expenditures over a period of five years from 2019.[22]

Even during India's G20 presidency, the issue of DRR and preparedness assumed great importance. India's G20 presidency built consensus to start a new work stream on DRR.

Prime Minister Narendra Modi sees disaster management as an international issue and not just a national or state-level issue. He has highlighted this at all international platforms; developed, developing, small or big—all nations have to come together to work on disaster management.

In recent years, India has proved to be a dependable first responder even for other countries. India was the single-most important responder during the Nepal earthquake. Even during the Turkey–Syria earthquake, India was one of the first to respond and contribute to the relief operations. India launched mission 'Operation Dost' by sending relief material and a full-fledged relief team including the Indian army, the NDRF units and medical teams along with equipment.[23]

Foreign Minister S. Jaishankar says that one major area where India's stature has rapidly increased in recent years is in terms of humanitarian assistance and relief provided to foreign nations at times of disasters. India has emerged as a first responder.[24]

When the nation faced an acute water crisis, Indian Navy was the first to arrive in the Maldives in 2014 and provide drinking water.[25] At the time of floods in Sri Lanka in 2017, India was the first responder.[26] In the floods of 2014, India offered a supporting hand to Pakistan.[27] During Covid-19, India launched Vaccine Maitri initiative to provide vaccines to poorer nations.[28]

SECURING THE FUTURE THROUGH TECHNOLOGY

At the NPDRR meeting of 2023, PM Modi mentioned, 'In Gujarat, there is a river in Kheda district which used to flood once in five–seven years. Once there were floods five times in one year, but a lot of initiatives had already been taken to manage this disaster. During then, simple mobile phones were available in every village. The system of messaging in local language was not developed. So, we sent Gujarati messages written in Roman script to the people, saying that there is a possibility of floods during these hours. And I clearly remember that even after five floods, let alone a human being, not even a single animal had died. Because we were able to communicate the information to the people timely.'[29]

PM Modi was stressing on the importance of technology. During floods in Surat in 2006, SMS messages sent in bulk prevented the loss of lives. In Kutch, he used the available technology to the optimum to increase awareness among people. Prime Minister Narendra Modi also mentioned how social media had immensely helped during the Mahi floods in Gujarat, adds Kamal Kishore from the NDMA. In the 10-point agenda of DRR, one of the points was about social media usage.

Prime Minister Narendra Modi has referred to the current decade as India's 'techade', during which the nation is expected to grow by leveraging technological advancement. He has been steering India's disaster risk apparatus to harness the latest advances in technology.[30] 'A roadmap should also be prepared after a comprehensive discussion on how we can make disaster management more responsive and effective with technologies like 5G, AI and IoT. How can we make the most out of drone technology in relief and rescue operations? Can we focus on such gadgets, which can alert us about the disaster or can give location information in case of anyone being buried under debris and about the person's position? We must focus on this kind of innovation. There are such social organizations in many countries of the world, which are creating new systems with the help of technology. We should also study them and adopt the best practices there,' PM Modi urged the stakeholders of Indian disaster management.[31]

Considering the future challenges, the PM has been steadily focussing on a greater level of capacity and preparedness, especially through the use of technology. He has encouraged the NDMA to adopt the latest and most efficient technology. 'We have released Common Alerting Protocol by the NDMA; this is a new technology and only five or six countries have it currently. His idea is to use indigenous and advanced technology to ensure safety of the people during disasters,' says Kishore.

The IDRN was catalogued across the nation and over 1 lakh new records were added in it. Systems like Disaster Management Information System Portal and 112 Emergency Response Support System were also set up.[32]

'Previously, our warnings would be delivered in English. Prime Minister Modi asked what the benefit was since most of the population did not understand the language. So, the warnings should go in Hindi and other vernacular languages,' says Kishore.

There is a greater focus on the use of technology, including space tech in the field of disaster management. The Indian Space Research Organisation (ISRO) identified wetlands in the

Northeast for flood management. Earlier, the IMD used to give a three-day advance forecast of rainfall. With the introduction of ISRO's space tech, the time of advance warnings improved to five days. In collaboration with ISRO, Forest Survey of India and the NDMA, an early detection system has been implemented. The PM, however, also insisted that whatever technology is used, the people should benefit from it.

'How will the people benefit? That is PM Modi's focus. For example, a person lives on the coastline of Odisha. If we make an early plan, will that person be able to receive information about it on time? Will he be able to get it in a way that he understands it? He always lays down emphasis on the use of our actions for the common man,' says Kishore.

Keeping this in mind, the NDMA has created a plethora of user-friendly solutions for helping people with right information at the right time, at any part of the country.

Prime Minister Narendra Modi understands that a vital component, almost a pre-requisite for the success of a disaster management mechanism, is the availability of adequate funding. He highlighted this when he allotted additional funds to Jammu & Kashmir during floods in 2014.

The prime minister is certainly one leader who was aware of the catastrophic conditions at the ground level after disasters. Naturally, his government consistently increased the funds available for this crucial domain.

The Indian states and local governments are provided with approximately $6 billion for disaster risk mitigation spanning five years (2021–25). In addition to this, there are resources amounting to $23 billion allocated for preparedness, response and recovery efforts.[33] Based on the recommendations of the 15th Finance Commission, the central government has allocated ₹1.28 trillion for State Disaster Response for the years 2021–22 to 2025–26, with the central government contributing ₹98,080.80 crore.[34]

On 13 June 2023, India's Union Home Minister Amit Shah launched a series of schemes to further strengthen the DRR apparatus. These included a ₹5,000-crore project to expand and modernize fire services across the states, a ₹2,500-crore project to reduce the risk of urban flooding in the seven most populous metros—Mumbai, Chennai, Kolkata, Bengaluru, Hyderabad, Ahmedabad and Pune—and ₹825 crore for National Landslide Risk Mitigation Project in 17 states and UTs.[35]

'Our approach towards disaster earlier was reactionary and relief-centric,' Shah said. He also added that from 2014 to 2023 the country had implemented on ground a new approach of early warning system, prevention, mitigation and preparedness-based disaster management. 'Budgetary provisions for disaster management have increased by 122% in the last eight years under the Modi government, which showed the priority given to it,' said the Union Home Minister.[36] The funds released to the NDRF and State Disaster Response Fund (SDRF) have tripled.[37]

Narendra Modi has consistently stressed on the significance of not only focusing on post-disaster response but also proactively preparing for possible events. 'As per the 15th Finance Commission recommendations, India's financial architecture disaster risk management covers a full circle of mitigation, preparedness, capacity building, response, recovery and reconstruction. This was not there earlier. Earlier we only focused on response after the disaster. The PM proactively worked in this area. This kind of arrangement is not there even in half a dozen countries. But it's there in India,' Kamal Kishore says.

So, from 2014 onwards, India aggressively moved forward to a state of greater preparedness on the basis of unique vision—focussing on long term resilience, while uniting the whole country and the world in pursuit of a safer planet.

Chapter 6

Saving a Billion Lives

INDIA'S COVID BATTLE

No other calamity had ever brought the world to its knees like the Covid-19 pandemic that originated in Wuhan, China, and rapidly made its way across the globe. Such was the impact of this virus that even the most powerful countries struggled helplessly to overcome it. However, India, a country often portrayed as one lacking in resources and expertise, stunned many an observer with its efficient handling of the situation.

The world's most populous country not only enforced effective lockdowns to curb the spread of the onslaught, it also managed to keep its economy on track. India was one of the few countries that manufactured not one but two incredibly effective vaccines—Covaxin and Covishield.

India rolled out the world's most expansive free vaccination drive for its entire population. In addition, countries that could not afford or were not capable of creating their vaccines also received these life-saving vaccines from India.

According to some estimates, people from over 100 countries have benefitted from made-in-India vaccines. However, despite the successes that India achieved in beating Covid-19, the onslaught was an extraordinary one. It was a frighteningly apocalyptic scenario that no one was prepared for. There were innumerable casualties. There was uncertainty, pain and all-pervasive gloom. Yet, the country endured it all and yet again showed its resilience.

QUICK RESPONSE

Even after Independence, India has seen massive natural calamities and underwent famines and more. Yet, what made the Covid-19 onslaught particularly ominous when it first hit the earth was its unpredictable nature. Nothing was known about the virus that was already killing people from China to Chile, Zambia and Zanzibar. No part of the world was immune.

All that was known was it had emanated in Wuhan in China and that there was no cure available for it. It was not known how deadly it was. During the initial days, even its mode of transmission mode was not known.

In India, the PM Modi's government decided to act swiftly and decisively from the moment inputs began pouring in about the Covid-19 pandemic. According to Rajiv Mehrishi, former Indian home secretary, the first high-level meeting to plan precautions for a possible outbreak was held under PM Modi in the beginning of January 2020. This was even before the first case in India was reported. The government began mulling a slew of measures, including screening of passengers at airports.

Many senior functionaries now recall with satisfaction that the country was quick to chart a course of action. The *Chalta Hai* attitude of the previous governments was non-existent in PM Modi's style of functioning.

Former Union Minister Prakash Javadekar says that the prime minister took note of the situation as soon as reports began emerging that Covid-19 situation was wreaking havoc in neighbouring China. 'When the first death in China was reported due to COVID, on 11 January 2020, PM Modi immediately sat with the Council of Ministers for a discussion. He said this was going to be a disastrous virus if we did not make preparations in advance,' says Javadekar.

Prime Minister Narendra Modi, who led the state of Gujarat through some of the most difficult times as its CM, gave a new disaster management paradigm as India made advance arrangements to meet the Covid-19 challenge. In the preceding chapters, one can observe how he had always been quick to react to situations, be it floods or earthquakes. This attribute now rubbed on to the central government. India, under him, responded with incredible alacrity to counter the pandemic. Quick response was one of the prime factors that helped India wade through the humongous Covid-19 crisis.

It was in January 2020 that the first case of Covid-19 was reported from the coastal state of Kerala. A 20-year-old student from Thrissur had come back from Wuhan and was found to be infected.[1] Covid-19 turned out to be a pandemic that travelled from country to country through airports.

The Indian government was quick to screen passengers at airports. Mechanisms were set up to quarantine infected passengers. Immediate measures were taken to isolate and treat them. The close contacts of the infected people were traced and monitored.

However, despite the plethora of urgent measures, Covid-19 proved to be highly contagious. The number of cases began to rise. In a matter of days, the cumulative figure of number of infected people had crossed a few hundreds. By the end of March 2020, the Covid-19 figure began to explode.

The virus had caught the world unaware. There were no proven techniques ready and available to test it. There was also much debate on how it spread.

The government was actively monitoring the situation at the highest levels. Meetings headed by PM Modi were being held regularly. Top experts were roped in and a high-level panel comprising experts in virology, epidemiology and public health was formed.

The Union health ministry began coordinating with states to ensure that India suffered minimum damage. Prime Minister Modi made it known to everyone in the government that tackling Covid-19 was his top priority.

'As early as 18th January 2020, when human-to-human transmission had not even been considered by WHO, we started screening Novel Coronavirus in our airports. We took proactive and pre-emptive actions,' says Former Union Health Secretary Preeti Sudan.

TO BE AWARE IS TO BE PROTECTED

An extraordinary achievement of PM Modi's government was that it could maintain trust among the people in this testing time, and it did so by ensuring transparent communication. The people understood the logic behind every tough decision that was being taken, and they agreed with the steps.

A massive awareness drive was initiated by the government. People were asked to follow social distancing, use masks and wash hands. India was one of the first countries that realized that awareness was the key to the battle against Covid-19. It utilized every media platform, from the conventional to the latest social media platforms.

Reviews of health facilities across the nation were conducted. All possible scenarios were evaluated and budgetary provisions for bridging the gaps were discussed. By March 2020, PM Modi and his team were well aware of the magnitude of the crisis. They started preparing the government for strong measures including the imposition of a lockdown.

Union Minister for Parliamentary Affairs Pralhad Joshi remembers his conversation with PM Modi. 'Around 18 March, he told me: "You might have to end the Parliament session early. Get the Finance Bill passed soon",' recalls Joshi.

Joshi was not yet aware of the seriousness of the situation. He asked the PM if he could get it done by 28 March. PM Modi replied that it may not be possible. 'The Covid-19 situation is not looking good. We will have to take some drastic measures. Talk to the opposition as well. We may have to close the session well before the date assigned,' Joshi recalls PM Modi telling him.

The former was curious and decided to ask the PM as to what was the likely solution to this calamity. Given India's huge population, the threat seemed huge. 'Vaccination is the only solution,' PM Modi told Joshi then and there. 'Prime Minister had started thinking about vaccines much earlier than everyone else,' Joshi says.

Prime Minister Narendra Modi began to engage with scientists to know how an antidote could be prepared. Decades of experience had taught him that in a calamitous situation, the administrator had to be nimble-footed. India could not wait for another country to manufacture a vaccine and then hand it over. Indians had to do it themselves, and the sooner the better.

India is one of the countries with the largest population. At the time of the Covid-19 outbreak, it was second to China. PM Modi's government decided to impose a lockdown in the nation with 1.3 billion-plus population. On 25 March 2020, the lockdown commenced. It was extended up to the end of May 2020 in four phases.[2]

'If the decision for lockdown in March was not taken, the

consequences would have been grave. The prime minister could take this early and bold decision,' says Mehrishi.

Experts and studies support the fact that an early lockdown helped India to a great extent. It slowed the pace of the onslaught of the unknown virus. It gave the authorities time to prepare. The provisions of the Disaster Management Act were invoked.

The imposition of lockdown was, however, quite challenging. PM Modi did it through persuasion, instead of force. To prepare the nation, PM Modi requested the nation to undergo a voluntary public curfew on 22 March 2020.[3] A master communicator, he made people aware of the dangers that the pandemic posed. From people in the remotest of villages to children in pre-school, everyone listened. Even as supposedly most advanced nations struggled, Indians managed to demonstrate amazing cohesiveness and ensured the success of lockdowns.

There were losses to businesses, and many faced financial challenges. The state and central governments did everything they could to alleviate their sufferings. However, it was a time when a tough and quick decision was needed for the well-being of the country. As a resolute leader, PM Modi could take the quick and proactive measures in face of one of the biggest catastrophes the modern world faced.

KEY TAKEAWAY

In situations of peril, hard decisions have to be taken. Implementing lockdowns was one such situation. However, rather than imposing them by force and creating chaos and dissent, a better way is to implement decisions through participation. The people need to be told that they would benefit from the move. Effective communication can take care of most issues that would otherwise arise while taking tough yet effective steps.

LEGAL BACKING

The Covid-19 scenario was an extraordinary one. Naturally, as pandemic spread, each country employed various legal mechanisms to address the crisis. India invoked the Disaster Management Act of 2005 and the Epidemic Diseases Act of 1897 as the primary legal frameworks. India also officially categorized the pandemic as a 'notified disaster' and efforts to curb it began on war footing.

Because of India's population, its healthcare infrastructure faces significant challenges even in the normal course of time. At a time when the country was grappling with a rapid surge of Covid-19, it became much more important that every resource at the disposal of the government was utilized to the optimum.

Covid-19 was declared as a 'notified disaster' so that assistance under the SDRF could be availed.[4] Formed under the Disaster Management Act of 2005, the SDRF is the primary fund available to the state governments for response to any disaster.

The Union Ministry of Home Affairs issued a notification on 14 March 2020, and it empowered states in managing the disaster. This was the first instance when the Disaster Management Act of 2005 was invoked.[5]

India provided a unique model in which the fight against Covid-19 was decentralized, yet incredibly coordinated at the same time. The strength of the country's federal model was visible to everyone. Despite political differences, overcoming the pandemic was the primary concern.

Under Section 6(2)(i) of the Disaster Management Act, the NDMA directed the National Executive Committee to issue guidelines to contain the epidemic. These guidelines acted as a compass that consistently provided a direction to the people. The NDMA issued an order on 23 March 2020, which instructed state governments to enact effective measures for containing the spread of Covid-19. In adherence to this order, the Ministry of Home Affairs promptly issued an order on the same day under Section 10(2)(l) of the Disaster Management Act, laying out guidelines and mandatory requirements for rigorous implementation. This order remained in effect for 21 days starting from 25 March 2020, marking the onset of India's initial nationwide Covid-19 lockdown.[6]

Sections 51–60 of the Disaster Management Act, 2005, were invoked to enforce the lockdown, which included offences and penalties for violations. Under these guidelines, public officials were also held accountable for the performance of their duties.[7]

Prime Minister Narendra Modi became the face of India's fight against Covid-19. He characterized India's response, and in it he involved the citizens to the maximum.

The PM's call for citizens to light lamps and torches during the early stages of the pandemic, symbolically combating the 'darkness' of the pandemic, reflects the government's inclusive approach. Frontline workers were hailed as 'Covid warriors'. The use of the term 'warrior' is significant as it made clear that the country was at battle against an unknown enemy that was spreading havoc indiscriminately.

In response to the Covid-19 pandemic, the Epidemic Diseases Act of 1897 was a crucial legal tool utilized by the Indian government. This Act grants the state governments the authority to implement special measures and regulations to prevent the spread of epidemic diseases. Under these provisions, the advisories issued by the Union health ministry were made legally enforceable.[8]

On 22 April 2020, the Epidemic Diseases (Amendment) Ordinance, 2020, was promulgated. This ordinance served as an amendment to the original Epidemic Diseases Act of 1897, specifically designed to combat the dissemination of dangerous epidemic diseases. Notably, this amendment introduced several changes to the Act, including provisions aimed at safeguarding healthcare personnel who were actively engaged in the battle against epidemic diseases.[9]

KEY TAKEAWAY

A proper classification of the disaster, supported by a robust legal framework ensures decentralized responses and swift implementation of measures. This enhances administrative accountability to the public, especially during health crises.

ATMANIRBHAR BHARAT—CONVERTING ADVERSITY TO OPPORTUNITY

The prime minister was steering India's efforts at a time when the country was on a path to building a strong health infrastructure. Unlike other politicians who may rue the absence of a magic wand, he decided to apply his mind to each and every challenge that the situation posed.

One key challenge was the need for protective gears that would save the workers, doctors, medical staff and others who were risking their lives in order to combat Covid-19. Personal protective equipment (PPE) is vital to keep doctors and medical staff, who treat Covid-19 patients, safe.

To get a sufficient number of PPE kits, N95 masks and other protective gear was a major task. Indian minister Smriti Irani was handling the textile portfolio. The key responsibility of procuring PPE kits fell in her domain. 'I recall that the textile ministry was under pressure as we had insufficient amount of PPE kits to sustain a long battle. India used to import 50,000–60,000 PPE suits every year as we did not have the raw material or machines. I remember PM Modi asking us if the suits could be made in India. We responded that we could develop it,' says Irani.

The Covid-19 menace was rising fast. It was estimated that the current stock of PPE suits in the nation would last only a month. PM Modi set a timeline to ensure that the country began producing quality PPE suits. However, there was a constraint in terms of availability of raw materials. The PM asked several ministries to work in tandem to overcome this challenge.

'He suggested that ministries work together to achieve it. In one instance, we talked to aviation minister Hardeep Puri to arrange special planes to bring in 30 PPE-manufacturing machines from Japan,' remembers Irani.

Prime Minister Narendra Modi had seen several crises and he knew how to turn a calamity into an opportunity. The manner in which India developed its capacity to produce PPE kits and N95 masks not only addressed the crisis but also strengthened the country's capacity to endure the Covid-19 pandemic. Considering the scale of the pandemic, there was a shortage of everything. From masks, sanitizers, PPE kits to oxygen cylinders, everything was needed in huge quantities.

Former chief of Defence Research and Development Organisation (DRDO), Satheesh Reddy recalls that, 'Along with mitigating the crisis, prime minister gave equal focus on *Atma Nirbharta*. He wanted India to be self-reliant regarding medical equipment. In such crises, a nation cannot depend on others.' He adds that, 'The DRDO was also involved in manufacturing many items including ventilators. PM Modi monitored the progress personally on a regular basis. With sanitizing equipment, high power RF-based sanitizers, airport scanning systems—there have been almost 75 products that were developed and more than 100 industries were given this technology overnight and they started producing all these things. Indian manufacturers also began to produce ventilators in thousands. A particularly challenging need was the production of medical oxygen. There was a technology developed by the DRDO, an on-board oxygen generation system for the TEJAS aircraft. During one of our meetings, the prime minister asked whether this can be modified into an oxygen plant and set up in All India Institute of Medical Sciences (AIIMS), Delhi. It was done in two weeks.'

With financial support from the PM CARES Fund, PM Modi gave similar targets to various organizations for the development of oxygen plants.[10] They were set up in almost every district of the country, including the Northeast[11] and Andaman Islands.[12] Agencies and manufacturers were asked to produce lightweight oxygen cylinders in bulk.

Prime Minister Narendra Modi kept pushing the country's scientists. He needed them to do more and more, and they responded with efficiency.

Covid-19 was also used as an opportunity to revamp India's health infrastructure, especially in Tier 2 and 3 cities and rural areas. During Covid-19, India scaled up its hospital infrastructure not only to meet the demands of the pandemic but also to face any health crisis in the future as well. Here, the concepts of 'Build Back Better' and 'Aapda me Avsar' made a discreet entry in India's fight. India's approach to create infrastructure that would immediately meet its short-term needs was quite visible. Even the DRDO was involved in the key tasks.

'Can you create makeshift hospitals, the PM asked us,' says Reddy. 'Make one in 10–15 days as a sample in Delhi, he suggested. The DRDO completed the task in almost 11 days, with 1,000 beds, ICU facilities, oxygen supply, etc.'

At the onset of the pandemic, India did not have the capacity to undertake millions of Covid-19 tests. However, the incredible part of India's journey was that the country managed to gain expertise, skills and facilities as it moved forward.

The network of laboratories was strengthened in the country. From one laboratory capable of testing for Covid-19 in January 2020, numbers rose to thousands, including in remote corners of the nation.[13] India developed indigenous testing kits and began manufacturing more than a million testing kits a day.[14]

More than anything else, it was clear in PM Modi's mind that India had to come up with its own vaccine, and preferably more than one vaccine, if the country has to emerge from the crisis. He put the entire expertise of the scientific community at the government's disposal so that India could produce its own vaccines. It did not matter if it was produced in the private or the public sector as long as it was Indian.

Dr N.K. Arora, former chairman of National Technical Advisory Group on Immunisation (NTAGI) says that in March 2020, planning for vaccine development started under PM Modi's leadership. At that time, the department of biotechnology sought proposals from different companies and scientists for manufacturing vaccines in India.

'In the month of February 2020, it was decided that the vaccine is the only solution to control the spread of Covid-19. Therefore, at the end of March, proposals were called,' Dr Arora says. 'Prime Minister Narendra Modi created the amalgamation of different experts, consultants, doctors, international consultants, scientific advisers, etc. The prime minister had said that India should not only emerge as a production hub for vaccines, but also be the leader in research and development of immunization technology,' he adds.

Former Indian Health Secretary Rajesh Bhushan recalls his team's meeting with PM Modi during the Covid-19 crisis. 'In August 2020, we were asked to form a group of experts who would decide on the rollout of the vaccine. He asked us about the best global practices.'

Various Indian companies were conducting research on their vaccines. PM Modi personally toured the facilities in Ahmedabad, Pune and Hyderabad to see the preparation and seek their opinion on how the government could help them further.[15]

'I believe it also played a significant role in how quickly different companies on different technological platforms worked on vaccines,' the former health secretary says.

The Indian scientific community rose up to the challenge and delivered multiple vaccines—Covaxin and Covishield became household names and a great accomplishment for India's scientific community.

Pankaj Patel, chairman of Zydus Lifesciences, recalls that PM Modi had sought his opinion on how the challenge should be addressed. The former responded that pharmaceutical companies like his could work on ensuring the availability of medicines of required quantities. PM Modi, however, was not satisfied. He wanted every Indian company to ramp up their production capacities not only to serve the needs of India, but also that of other nations who needed India's help.

Prime Minister Narendra Modi used Covid-19 as an Aapda me Avsar[16] instance of disaster management, a concept which he carries along since Morbi and Kutch, for augmenting India's health infrastructure and capacity.

COLLECTIVE EFFORT

Covid-19 also was a test of India's collective spirit, which underlies the disaster management paradigm advocated by PM Modi all these years.

PM Modi brought the entire team together including union ministers, secretaries, government institutions, public sector undertakings (PSUs), state governments, scientists, health experts, defence forces, etc. A strong believer in team work, he knew that silos had to be broken. Most importantly, he made the people of India a key stakeholder. 'India's Covid-19 fight is people driven and gets great strength from our Covid warriors. Our collective efforts have helped saved many lives,' PM Modi said in a social media post.[17]

Before the announcement of the lockdown, PM Modi urged the people to observe a voluntary *Janata Curfew* on Sunday, 22 March 2020. It was a very interesting choice of words. A curfew imposed by the people for themselves. He has seen even tough times like the Emergency. In a democracy, the strongest force is always the will of the people. He, from the very beginning, was very sure of making the fight against Covid-19 a Jan Andolan. On the day of the curfew, acting on PM Modi's call, people clapped, drummed kitchen utensils and even blew conches to honour those on the frontline battling the deadly virus. This in turn also lifted the national morale.

Meanwhile, the government rolled out innovative campaigns to make people aware of the crisis and the steps needed to stay safe. '*Do gaj ki doori hai zaroori*', translated in English as 'a two-yard distance is a must for safety', became a mantra. Social distancing became the norm across the country. All these efforts from the government ensured that a billion people follow Covid appropriate behaviour, and the results of the efforts of a united India began to surprise everyone. Experts in the West often liked to think of India as a poor, backward country struggling with its problems. Meanwhile, India was putting up a bold fight when the rest of the world was struggling, riding on the strength of people's power.

Prime Minister Narendra Modi continued to communicate closely with the people. He issued another appeal as April arrived. 'I want nine minutes from you on 5th April, Sunday. Switch off all the lights in your homes, come to the door or the balcony and light a candle or switch on the torchlight on your phones,' he said.[18] The innovative manner in which India was handling Covid-19 was surprising for not just those abroad, even those who had seen the inefficiency of past governments found the initiatives remarkable.

Another aspect of the movement led by PM Modi was the collective involvement of everyone, each contributing their bit. While the medical community was taking care of people and the scientific community was developing vaccines, millions of other Indians were making their own contributions.

Well-meaning Indians from all spheres of life were making handsome contributions to the PM CARES Fund. It received a total of ₹12,691.82 crore as voluntary contributions in three years from 2020 to 2022.[19] From prominent sportspersons, film stars and industrialists to children who broke their piggybanks to contribute to PM CARES Fund, everyone did their bit.

During the early stages of the lockdown, there was a pressing requirement to manage the pandemic effectively, all the while guaranteeing fundamental welfare and food security for the populace. The central government, under the auspices of the NDMA, released directives to state and district authorities, outlining specific measures to be carried out by local bodies like panchayats, as well as healthcare and community personnel. The primary focus was on containing the transmission of the virus among returning migrants.

In pursuit of this goal, panchayats were directed to collaborate with frontline healthcare workers such as Accredited Social Health Activists (ASHA), Auxiliary Nurse Midwives (ANM), women Self-Help Groups (SHGs), local community stakeholders including teachers, and various others. This collaborative effort was facilitated through the establishment of committees at the panchayat or village level, which went by different names in different states. Local-level administration has turned out to be instrumental in the last-mile delivery of Covid-related measures.[20]

PM Modi's government, through the NDMA, brought about a redefinition of established institutional roles in response to the Covid-19 pandemic. This comprehensive strategy led to the integration of numerous institutional entities spanning state, district and local administrations.

To handle the Covid-19 outbreak, PM Modi incorporated several empowered groups, headed by senior officials. The management of the Covid-19 scenario became his foremost priority and the entire government participated towards it. The empowered groups constituted on 29 March 2020 addressed issues like medical emergency planning; availability of hospitals, isolation and quarantine facility; disease surveillance and testing; ensuring availability of essential medical equipment; augmenting human resource and capacity building; supply chain and logistics management; coordination with private sector; economic and welfare measures; information, communications and public awareness; technology and data management; public grievances and suggestions; and strategic issues related to lockdown.[21]

Apart from these, hundreds of meetings and several video conferences were held by the prime minister in all the states. The GoI provided the state governments and UT administrations with needed plans and procedures. The PM bridged gap between departments and ministries. He ushered in an unconventional approach.

'Prime Minister Narendra Modi knew how capacities of various departments could have been used for disaster management. For instance, the DRDO might not have imagined that they could be of this use in handling Covid-19,' says NDMA member secretary Kamal Kishore.

This innovative approach was visible in the manner in which the assets of the railways were used. Former railway board chairman Vinod Yadav recalls, 'During the outbreak of Covid-19, there was a scarcity of hospital beds. A group was formed to monitor the development of the hospital's infrastructure, and I was also part of that. The major problem was in rural areas where there was no sufficient infrastructure. It was a challenge to transport patients in critical conditions from rural areas to hospitals in urban centres. PM Modi gave a solution to that problem in a meeting. He said, "Railway can reach anywhere, so why don't you think about converting railway coaches into isolation units?" Then railway coaches were converted where there were shortages of beds.'

In the beginning of March 2020, seven ministries were tasked with setting up quarantine facilities for patients and helping in the treatment. Thirteen other ministries were also asked to collaborate in other related activities.[22] Every possible department was involved in the process. Various committees of experts were formed to suggest effective and fast response measures. An Economic Response Task Force was also formed with the objective of minimizing the economic impact of Covid-19. A collective effort was initiated even before the lockdown in March 2020.

The National Expert Group on Vaccine Administration for Covid-19 guided every aspect of vaccine rollout in India. It had high-level coordination with 19 ministries at the national level and 23 departments at the state and district levels, with numerous developmental partners.[23]

Furthermore, PM Modi led from the front. He was available in most of the high-level meetings. He regularly interacted with experts, scientists, industry officials, and so on. He was also available to the people of the nation to maintain their confidence.

'Prime Minister Narendra Modi may have held more than 25 meetings with state chief ministers alone during Covid-19 pandemic,' says former Indian Health Secretary Rajesh Bhushan.

Another success was the vaccination drive of more than a billion people. Everyone came forward voluntarily and lakhs of health workers gave their services for months to administer Covid-19 vaccines to all Indians. As of March 2023, India has administered 2.2 billion doses of vaccines.[24]

The government also launched a massive Vande Bharat Mission on 7 May 2020 to bring home stranded Indians from foreign countries due to Covid-19 pandemic.[25]

KEY TAKEAWAY

Covid-19 underlines the necessity of a disaster management model based on people's participation and collaboration. Along with scaling up capacities in terms of infrastructure and technology, human resource capacity building should be an essential component of the strategy towards preparedness.

SAFEGUARDING THE POOR

The toughest blow of Covid-19 was being inflicted upon the poor and the economically backward. Not only were they vulnerable to the ominous infection, their livelihoods were also being crushed. Those who lived from hand-to-mouth could have found it extremely difficult to survive in prolonged period of lockdowns.

A slew of schemes were initiated to ensure that the poor and the needy were taken care of. The scale of these programmes was unprecedented. For instance, under the Pradhan Mantri Garib Kalyan Package of ₹1.70 lakh crore, free food grain for 80 crore people, free cooking gas for 8 crore families and direct cash transfer to over 40 crore needy people were provided.[26] This was by far one of the largest programmes of its kind. This provided the much-needed succour to these families. In addition, under Pradhan Mantri Garib Kalyan Rojgar Abhiyan, 50.78 crore person-days of employment was generated incurring an expenditure of ₹39,293 crore.[27] Health workers were provided insurance cover of ₹50 lakhs.[28]

The government was also working to ensure that small entrepreneurs and businesses also could stay afloat. The government undertook countless measures with each passing day to support livelihood like, ₹3 lakh crore collateral-free automatic loans for small businesses, ₹50,000 crore equity infusion through the Ministry of Micro, Small & Medium Enterprises (MSME) Fund, new revised criteria for classification of the MSMEs, Emergency Credit Line Guarantee Scheme (ECLGS) and so on.[29]

The MSMEs were not allowed to go bankrupt with the help of loan disbursals worth ₹3.5 lakh crore.[30] The government sought to provide a healing touch to those who had suffered during the pandemic by launching various schemes.

A FRIEND IN TECHNOLOGY

PM Modi's initiatives in the battle against Covid-19 showcased a comprehensive approach that harnessed technology and innovation. India developed indigenous vaccines, online platforms streamlined vaccination processes and helped in monitoring the spread. The nation established genomic surveillance to monitor and respond to virus variants effectively.

India could develop indigenous vaccines within a short period of time and do mass production, so as to cater to the large population. India's vaccine technology resulted in a diverse vaccine arsenal and placed India in a secure position to combat viruses effectively. Prime Minister Narendra Modi's government launched Mission COVID Suraksha to develop the vaccines and provided a special package for the technology development.[31]

Newer technologies of vaccine including the mRNA technology were developed by Indian scientists. [32]

One significant achievement was the establishment of genomic surveillance, a system designed to track the variants of the virus by tracing gene samples within the community. This surveillance, initiated in December 2020, enabled the identification of various Covid-19 variants, including Alpha, Delta and Omicron. This mechanism facilitated the monitoring of the virus and the development of vaccines tailored to its specific strains. Furthermore, it paved the way for a network of over 50 laboratories to detect and diagnose various viruses in the country, enabling timely and effective responses.

Prime Minister Narendra Modi played a crucial role in the development of the CoWIN portal. The groundwork for this platform began in July–August 2020 with the aim of efficiently tracking the vaccination of India's vast population of 1.25 billion people. It evolved to provide vaccination certificates that include details about the administered doses, the administering personnel and the timing.[33] This system introduced a rare level of accountability, garnering global recognition and appreciation for India's vaccination programme. This end-to-end solution efficiently managed tasks like registration, appointment scheduling, identity verification, vaccination and certification, ensuring resource efficiency and improved vaccine accessibility.

In addition to the introduction of the CoWIN portal, PM Modi's leadership spurred the utilization of several other critical technologies. The Electronic Vaccine Intelligence Network (eVIN) played a crucial role in establishing a robust vaccine supply chain. The Digital Infrastructure for Vaccination Open Credentialing (DIVOC) facilitated the issuance of digitally verifiable vaccination certificates. The Surveillance and Action for Events Following Vaccination (SAFE-VAC) system effectively tracked adverse events following immunization. These technologies, guided by PM Modi's vision, boasted a scalable architecture that allowed the success of vaccination of over 25 million people in a single day.[34]

Additionally, the Aarogya Setu mobile app, introduced in April 2020 soon after the outbreak, proved to be a critical tool. It employed technology, such as Bluetooth-based contact tracing, to record interactions with other individuals. The app provided real-time alerts to individuals who came into contact with a Covid-positive person and disseminated essential advisories following the Ministry of Health and Family Welfare (MoHFW) and the Indian Council of Medical Research (ICMR) guidelines.[35]

Technology was used extensively in monitoring the availability of oxygen across the nation, even to track the movement of oxygen cylinders. Apart from all these, technology was leveraged to the optimum for easing the life of people as well as restoring livelihoods. Online tools for web conferencing, digital payments, online health consultation and virtual classrooms were a few areas where the government put extra effort into building new capabilities.

Covid-19, however, has shaken the world to its core. Many countries staged remarkable recoveries. India's fight was definitely one of the toughest and one of the most extraordinary. It was a fight that generations will remember and can be proud of.

The pandemic was relentless. So were the PM Modi's government's efforts to mitigate the challenges. It revealed the innate resilience of the nation and augmented India's disaster management capabilities.

The nation's disaster management mechanism received a paradigm shift in the last 10 years of PM Modi's government. India has marched a long way forward to become a resilient nation and a global leader in disaster management.

Notes

Introduction

1. 'Unstarred Question No. 1238', *Ministry of Home Affairs, Government of India,* https://tinyurl.com/ddzbvxb9. Accessed on 3 January 2023.
2. Mishra, Pramod K., *The Kutch Earthquake 2001: Recollections, Lessons and Insights*, National Institute of Disaster Management, New Delhi.

Chapter 1: The Tears of Morbi 1979

1. PTI, 'Tsunami 2004: Tamil Nadu Remembers Victims on 18th Anniversary', *The Times of India*, 26 December 2022, https://tinyurl.com/29zwswpd. Accessed on 20 October 2023.
2. TNN, 'In Last 20 Years, 2 Earthquakes Have Claimed over 2 Lakh Lives Each', *The Times of India,* 10 February 2023, https://tinyurl.com/4ft7hms2. Accessed on 20 October 2023.
3. 'Machchu Dam 2 near Morbi', *morbionline.in,* https://tinyurl.com/4f35d3k8. Accessed on 20 October 2023.
4. Easwaran, S.B., 'The Loudest Crash of '79', *Outlook*, 5 February 2022, https://tinyurl.com/2s3v64pm. Accessed on 20 October 2023.
5. 'National Disaster Response Force', *Ministry of Home Affairs, Government of India,* https://tinyurl.com/zz674c8m. Accessed on 1 November 2023.
6. 'Aapda Mitra', *National Disaster Management Authority, Government of India,* https://tinyurl.com/5bmwe3t4. Accessed on 2 November 2023.
7. 'PM Modi Addresses Public Meeting in Morbi, Gujarat', *YouTube,* https://tinyurl.com/4ccxb8rc. Accessed on 20 October 2023.
8. Mehta, Nalini, 'When Narendra Modi First Appeared in the Newspapers', *The Times of India,* https://tinyurl.com/3y5um3dy. Accessed on 20 October 2023.
9. Sandesara, Utpal, and Tom Wooten, *No One Had a Tongue to Speak: The Untold Story of One of Historys Deadliest Floods*, Rain Tree, 2012.
10. Chawla, Mayank, 'Another Morbi Tragedy: World's Deadliest Dam Disaster

Killed 2,000 in 1979', *The Quint,* 10 November 2022, https://tinyurl.com/yayc5255. Accessed on 1 November 2023.

11. 'Cholera in Haiti', *Centers for Disease Control and Prevention,* https://tinyurl.com/4zw6b3vn. Accessed on 20 October 2023.
12. Chawla, Mayank, 'Another Morbi Tragedy: World's Deadliest Dam Disaster Killed 2,000 in 1979', *The Quint,* 10 November 2022, https://tinyurl.com/yayc5255. Accessed on 23 October 2023.
13. 'Vice President to Inaugurate International Conference on Dam Safety at Jaipur, Rajasthan on 14th September, 2023', *PIB.gov,* 12 September 2023, https://tinyurl.com/6srdhn3a. Accessed on 23 October 2023.
14. 'Bill Provides for Adequate Surveillance, Inspection, Operation & Maintenance of All Large Dams in the Country So as to Prevent Dam Failure Related Disasters', *PIB.gov,* 2 December 2021, https://tinyurl.com/3zy3asy6. Accessed on 23 October 2023.

Chapter 2: Devastation in Kutch

1. 'Bhuj Earthquake of 2001', *Britannica,* 29 September 2023, https://tinyurl.com/ye9kntt2. Accessed on 23 October 2023.
2. Mishra, Pramod K., *The Kutch Earthquake 2001: Recollections, Lessons and Insights,* National Institute of Disaster Management, New Delhi.
3. Ibid.
4. Pearn, Edward, et al., 'United Nations Disaster Assessment and Co-ordination (UNDAC) Team Bhuj Final Report', *reliefweb,* 20 February 2001, https://tinyurl.com/mr2r4j3b. Accessed on 23 October 2023.
5. Mishra, Pramod K., *The Kutch Earthquake 2001: Recollections, Lessons and Insights,* National Institute of Disaster Management, New Delhi.
6. Patra, Debabrat, and Aditi Roy, 'Why Women Need to Be at the Heart of Disaster Response: Lessons from Odisha Super Cyclone', *DownToEarth,* 24 July 2023, https://tinyurl.com/3xb9kwkp. Accessed on 23 October 2023.
7. Sharma, Rishabh, 'As Biparjoy Hits Gujarat, a Look at How Odisha Became Role Model in Cyclone Management', *India Today,* 28 July 2023, https://tinyurl.com/sfkuz9zp. Accessed on 30 October 2023.
8. Pandher, Sarabjit, 'Modi, Bjp Brass Attend Khattar Swearing-in', *The Hindu,* 26 October 2014, https://tinyurl.com/3js5zmn9. Accessed on 23 October 2023.

Chapter 3: Kutch Bounces Back

1. *Gujarat Earthquake Reconstruction and Rehabilitation Policy,* The Gujarat State Disaster Management Authority, Gujarat, December 2001.

2. Ibid.
3. *From Relief to Recovery: The GUJARAT Experience*, United Nations Development Programme, 24 May 2012.
4. *India: Gujarat Earthquake Rehabilitation and Reconstruction Project,* Asian Development Bank, 2008
5. Mishra, Pramod K., *The Kutch Earthquake 2001: Recollections, Lessons and Insights*, National Institute of Disaster Management, New Delhi.
6. Sakuntala, Narasimhan, Lessons from Latur: A Decade after the Earthquake, Economic and Political Weekly, pp. 4730-732.
7. Mishra, Pramod K., *The Kutch Earthquake 2001: Recollections, Lessons and Insights*, National Institute of Disaster Management, New Delhi.
8. Ibid.
9. 'Development of Kutch Is a Perfect Example of a Meaningful Change with "Sabka Prayas": PM', *Narendra Modi,* 28 August 2022, https://tinyurl.com/r3e4smnz. Accessed on 1 November 2023.
10. *From Relief to Recovery: The GUJARAT Experience*, United Nations Development Programme, 24 May 2012.
11. 'The Particulars of Organization, Functions and Duties: Gujarat State Disaster Management Authority', *Gujarat State Disaster Management Authority*, https://tinyurl.com/2h6rz448. Accessed on 27 October 2023.
12. PTI, 'Relief in Sales Tax for Kutch Industries', *The Times of India,* 5 November 2001, https://tinyurl.com/2hmp9nyt. Accessed on 1 November 2023.
13. Mishra, Pramod K., *The Kutch Earthquake 2001: Recollections, Lessons and Insights*, National Institute of Disaster Management, New Delhi.
14. *From Relief to Recovery: The GUJARAT Experience*, United Nations Development Programme, 24 May 2012.
15. Vora, Rutam, 'Modi Recounts Kutch's Post-earthquake Development, Which Became the Flagbearer of Gujarat's Economic Growth', *The Hindu Businessline*, 29 August 2022, https://tinyurl.com/kvppaw8n. Accessed on 24 October 2023.
16 Lal, Preeti Verma, 'Dhordo, Winner of UNWTO's Best Tourism Village Award, is Ready for Rann Utsav', *Hindustan Times*, 26 October 2023, https://tinyurl.com/e2rr45v6. Accessed on 8 November 2023.
17. 'Know Why 'Kutch Nahin Dekha Toh Kuch Ni Dekha'?', *Kutch Tour Guide*, 29 December 2016, https://tinyurl.com/9yf978ea. Accessed on 24 October 2023.
18. PTI, 'Unesco Heritage Award for Gujarat Sikh Shrine', *Hindustan Times*, 2 June 2005, https://tinyurl.com/yc7xyf2x. Accessed on 24 October 2023.
19. *From Relief to Recovery:* The GUJARAT Experience, United Nations Development Programme.

Chapter 4: Mission Preparedness

1. *HYOGO FRAMEWORK FOR ACTION 2005-2015: Building the Resilience of Nations and Communities to Disasters*, United Nations International Strategy for Disaster Reduction, 2005.
2. Ibid.
3. *Gujarat Earthquake Reconstruction and Rehabilitation Policy*, The Gujarat State Disaster Management Authority, Gujarat, December 2001.
4. Sharma, Rishabh, 'As Biparjoy Hits Gujarat, a Look at How Odisha Became Role Model in Cyclone Management', *India Today,* 28 July 2023, https://tinyurl.com/sfkuz9zp. Accessed on 30 October 2023.
5. 'Earthquake', *Gujarat State Disaster Management Authority*, https://tinyurl.com/yc3xeps8. Accessed on 31 October 2023.
6. TNN, 'Gujarat Bags UN Award for Disaster Management', *The Times of India*, 22 October 2023, https://tinyurl.com/3wnyxzxb. Accessed on 25 October 2023.
7. 'Welcome to Gujarat State Disaster Management', *GSDMA,* https://tinyurl.com/2s2xpbe8. Accessed on 11 November 2023.
8. Gujarat State Disaster Management Act, 2003', *Gujarat State Disaster Management Authority*, https://tinyurl.com/y2csvwds. Accessed on 31 October 2023.
9. Ibid.
10. Chih-Chieh Lu, et al., 'Anti-Liquefaction Mechanisms in Buildings with Shallow Foundations with a Focus on Lowering the Ground Water Table', *Soil Dynamics and Earthquake Engineering*, Volume 175, 2023, 108275.
11. Mishra, Pramod K., *The Kutch Earthquake 2001: Recollections, Lessons and Insights*, National Institute of Disaster Management, New Delhi.
12. 'Shri Narendra Modi at Int'l Conference on Post Earthquake Reconstruction at PDPU', YouTube, https://tinyurl.com/y7d7pe2k. Accessed on 25 October 2023.
13. 'About ISR', *Institute of Seismological Research, Government of Gujarat*, https://tinyurl.com/499cc8m2. Accessed on 27 October 2023.
14. Broughton, Edward, 'The Bhopal Disaster and Its Aftermath: A Review', *Environmental Health*, Volume 4, 2005.
15. 'State Level Chemical & Industrial Disaster Management Plan', *Gujarat State Disaster Management Authority,* https://tinyurl.com/52cbyhpa. Accessed on 31 October 2023.
16. 'Action Plan for Nuclear & Radiological Disaster', *Gujarat State Disaster Management Authority*, https://tinyurl.com/ycks6u2a. Accessed on 31 October 2023.

17. 'About GSWAN', *Gujarat State Wide Area Network,* https://tinyurl.com/2p8xn7s6. Accessed on 31 October 2023.
18. Singh, Dhirendra Pratap, 'Why Gujarat Leads India', *eGov Magazine,* 10 December 2011, https://tinyurl.com/43f4npsc. Accessed on 31 October 2023.
19. *EGram Vishwagram Project,* https://tinyurl.com/y2enc7yn. Accessed on 31 October 2023.
20. 'State Disaster Resource Network', *Gujarat State Disaster Management Authority,* https://tinyurl.com/bdd68xcj. Accessed on 31 October 2023.
21. 'Towards a Disaster Resilient Community in Gujarat', *GoI-UNDP Disaster Risk Management Programme,* https://tinyurl.com/2vmhen52. Accessed on 31 October 2023.
22. Kumar, Rajendra, 'An Overview of DARMAT', *Collectorate of Rajkot,* https://tinyurl.com/2pbmau77. Accessed on 31 October 2023.
23. 'Hazard Risk and Vulnerability Assessment (HRVA)', *Gujarat State Disaster Management Authority,* https://tinyurl.com/2rbypmm5. Accessed on 31 October 2023.
24. Khanna, Sumit, and Sudipto Ganguly, 'India Cyclone: Casualties Averted with Early Warnings and Timely Evacuation', *Reuters,* 16 June 2023, https://tinyurl.com/r2njbj2x. Accessed on 25 October 2023.
25. News9Live Staff, 'Ukai Dam: All You Need to Know about Gujarat's Second-Largest Reservoir', *Newsnine,* 23 September 2022, https://tinyurl.com/398p468e. Accessed on 31 October 2023.
26. Parikh, Kirit, et al., 'Vulnerability of Surat, Gujarat to Flooding from Tapi River: A Climate Change Impact Assessment', *Vayu Mandal,* Volume 43, Issue 2, 2017m 120–9.
27. Mavalankar, Dileep, and Amit Srivastava, 'Lessons from Massive Floods of 2006 in Surat City: A Framework for Application of MS/OR Techniques to Improve Dam Management to Prevent Flood', IIMA Working Papers WP2008-07-06, Indian Institute of Management Ahmedabad, https://tinyurl.com/54vm2k4m. Accessed on 7 November 2023.
28. 'Surat Floods Commission Gives Clean Chit to Administration', *Oneindia,* 29 September 2008, https://tinyurl.com/yd9sabbn. Accessed on 25 October 2023.

Chapter 5: The Making of a Resilient Nation

1. 'Gujarat State Disaster Management Act, 2003', *Gujarat State Disaster Management Authority,* https://tinyurl.com/y2csvwds. Accessed on 27 October 2023.

2. *Report of the Comptroller and Auditor General of India on Performance Audit of Disaster Preparedness in India*, Union Government (Civil), Ministry of Home Affairs, 2013.
3. Tripathi, Rahul, 'Cabinet to Take Up Proposal to Amend Disaster Management Act', *The Economic Times*, 25 January 2020, https://tinyurl.com/bdf8cskp. Accessed on 25 October 2023.
4. Aurora, Bhavna, 'Prime Minister Narendra Modi to Spend Diwali with Jammu and Kashmir Flood Victims', *The Economic Times*, 22 October 2014, https://tinyurl.com/3paytf2u. Accessed on 25 October 2023.
5. 'PM Modi's Mann ki Baat: As It Happened on April 26, 2015', *Zee News*, 27 April 2005, https://tinyurl.com/3waaby4f. Accessed on 25 October 2023
6. 'Prime Minister Shri Narendra Modi's "Mann KI Baat" on 29 November, 2015', YouTube, https://tinyurl.com/3smtdpvw. Accessed on 25 October 2023.
7. Watwani, Jigyasa, 'India Releases First Ever National Disaster Management Plan', *DownToEarth*, 2 June 2016, https://tinyurl.com/2se8ttby. Accessed on 25 October 2023.
8. 'What Is the Sendai Framework for Disaster Risk Reduction?', *United Nations Office for Disaster Risk Reduction*, https://tinyurl.com/3rzpbvt9. Accessed on 25 October 2023.
9. 'Based on 15th Finance Commission Recommendations, Central Government Has Allocated Rs. 32,031 Crore for SDMF and Rs. 13,693 Crore for National Disaster Mitigation Fund (NDMF) For the Years 2021-22 to 2025-26', *Ministry of Home Affairs, Government of India*, 30 September 2022, https://tinyurl.com/bp5tt2p7. Accessed on 25 October 2023.
10. PTI, 'Encourage Leadership of Women in Disaster Risk Management: PM Modi', *NDTV*, 3 November 2016, https://tinyurl.com/46js52wv. Accessed on 25 October 2023.
11. 'Prime Minister's Address at Asian Ministerial Conference on Disaster Risk Reduction', Press Information Bureau, 3 November 2016, https://tinyurl.com/bdfct76d. Accessed on 31 October 2023.
12. 'In India, We Are Committed to Walk the Talk on the Implementation of Sendai Framework: PM Modi', *Narendra Modi*, 3 November 2016, https://tinyurl.com/35k9uj26. Accessed on 31 October 2023.
13. 'Prime Minister's Ten Point Agenda on DRR', *National Disaster Management Authority, Government of India*, https://tinyurl.com/3ajbtasw. Accessed on 25 October 2023.
14. 'PM's Address at Asian Ministerial Conference on Disaster Risk Reduction', *PMINDIA*, 3 November 2016, https://tinyurl.com/29hn34nd. Accessed on 9 November 2023.

15. 'Aapda Mitra', *National Disaster Management Authority, Goventment of India*, https://tinyurl.com/5bmwe3t4. Accessed on 2 November 2023.
16. 'PM Unveils Hologram Statue of Netaji at India Gate', *Press Information Bureau, Government of India*, 23 January 2022, https://tinyurl.com/5yscvktm. Accessed on 25 October 2023.
17. 'PM Modi Inaugurates National Platform for Disaster Risk Reduction (NPDRR) Delhi on March 10, 2023', YouTube, https://tinyurl.com/2etcn723. Accessed on 25 October 2023.
18. 'English Rendering of PM's Address at 3rd Meeting of NPDRR & Subhash Chandra Bose Aapda Prabandhan Puraskar-2023', *Press Information Bureau, Government of India*, 10 March 2023, https://tinyurl.com/4uy9c443. Accessed on 25 October 2023.
19. Ibid.
20. 'Odisha State Disaster Management Authority and Lunglei Fire Station, Mizoram, Selected in the Institutional Category for Subhash Chandra Bose Aapda Prabandhan Puraskar-2023', *Press Information Bureau, Government of India*, 23 January 2023, https://tinyurl.com/4ctzjwj9. Accessed on 25 October 2023.
21. 'Members', *Coalition for Disaster Resilient Infrastructure,* https://tinyurl.com/y9vuyuct. Accessed on 31 October 2023.
22. 'Cabinet Approves Categorization of the Coalition for Disaster Resilient Infrastructure (CDRI) As an "International Organization" and Signing of the Headquarters Agreement (HQA) With CDRI for Granting It the Exemptions, Immunities and Privileges as Contemplated under the United Nations (Privileges & Immunities) Act, 1947', *Press Information Bureau, Government of India*, 29 June 2022, https://tinyurl.com/53w6nrkt. Accessed on 25 October 2023.
23. 'Union Home Minister and Minister of Cooperation Shri Amit Shah Chaired the Meeting of Heads of Departments of Shanghai Cooperation Organization (SCO) Member States Responsible for Prevention and Elimination of Emergency Situations, in New Delhi Today', *Press Information Bureau, Government of India*, 20 April 2023, https://tinyurl.com/27jm9jk6. Accessed on 26 October 2023.
24. 'India's Statement Delivered by the External Affairs Minister, Dr. S. Jaishankar at the General Debate of the 77th Session of the UN General Assembly', *Ministry of External Affairs Government of India*, 25 September 2022, https://tinyurl.com/52x6dw7b. Accessed on 26 October 2023.
25. ANI, 'Indian Navy First to Respond and Help Crisis-Hit Maldives', *Business Standard,* 7 December 2014, https://tinyurl.com/3prew3mx. Accessed on 30 October 2023.

26. 'Responding First as a Leading Power', *Ministry of External Affairs Government of India,* https://tinyurl.com/pfsyt67p. Accessed on 31 October 2023.
27. PTI, 'PM Narendra Modi Offers Assistance to Pakistan for Relief Operations in Flood-Hit PoK', *The Economic Times,* 7 September 2014, https://tinyurl.com/3hdt67mm. Accessed on 31 October 2023.
28. Sharma, Jyoti, and S.K. Varshney, 'India's Vaccine Diplomacy Aids Global Access to COVID-19 Jabs', *Nature India,* 17 February 2021, https://tinyurl.com/22f99zbv. Accessed on 2 November 2023.
29. 'English Rendering of PM's Address at 3rd Meeting of NPDRR & Subhash Chandra Bose Aapda Prabandhan Puraskar-2023', *PIB.gov.in,* 10 March 2023, https://tinyurl.com/4msy8dae. Accessed on 9 November 2023.
30. PTI, 'This Decade Will Be 'India's Techade', Says PM Modi', *The Hindu,* 1 July 2021, https://tinyurl.com/56ypzww8. Accessed on 26 October 2023.
31. 'English Rendering of PM's Address at 3rd Meeting of NPDRR & Subhash Chandra Bose Aapda Prabandhan Puraskar-2023', *Nature India,* 10 March 2023, https://tinyurl.com/4msy8dae. Accessed on 26 October 2023.
32. 'Union Home Minister and Minister of Cooperation, Shri Amit Shah Chairs a Meeting with Ministers of Disaster Management of the States/ Union Territories, at Vigyanbhawan in New Delhi, Today', *Nature India,* 13 June 2023, https://tinyurl.com/ystkr72y. Accessed on 30 October 2023.
33. 'Midterm Review of Sendai Framework for Disaster Risk Reduction (2015-2030)', *Prime Minister's Office,* 18 May 2023, https://tinyurl.com/3xvxvuz6. Accessed on 30 October 2023.
34. 'Centre Approves Release of ₹7,532 Crore to 22 States under Disaster Response Fund', *Mint,* 12 July 2023, https://tinyurl.com/n5fj85wn. Accessed on 30 October 2023.
35. DHNS, 'Amit Shah Unveils Rs 8K-Cr Projects for Disaster Management', *Deccan Herald,* 13 June 2023, https://tinyurl.com/3fk3fzhc. Accessed on 26 October 2023.
36. 'Under Narendra Modi, Disaster Management Allocation Rose by 122%: Amit Shah', *The Times of India,* 26 June 2022, https://tinyurl.com/4vbs44zx. Accessed on 26 October 2023.
37. 'Home Minister Amit Shah Chairs Meeting to Make India Disaster-Resilient', *Public TV,* 13 June 2023, https://tinyurl.com/55vwvc59. Accessed on 26 October 2023.

Chapter 6: Saving A Billion Lives

1. Ghosh, Abantika, 'First Positive Corona Case Is Wuhan Medical Student from Kerala', *The Indian Express*, 31 January 2020, https://tinyurl.com/46sfw7zr. Accessed on 26 October 2023.
2. 'Coronavirus in India: 21-Day Lockdown Begins; Key Highlights of PM Modi's Speech', *Business Today*, 25 March 2020, https://tinyurl.com/2hk8er7v. Accessed on 26 October 2023.
3. PTI, 'India to Observe "Janata Curfew" on Sunday amid Spurt in Coronavirus Cases', *The Economic Times*, 22 March 2020, https://tinyurl.com/4u47r539. Accessed on 26 October 2023.
4. 'India Declares Coronavirus Outbreak as a Notified Disaster', 14 March 2020, *Mint*, https://tinyurl.com/2p969unb. Accessed on 26 October 2023.
5. Chauhan, Chetan, 'COVID-19: Disaster Act Invoked for the 1st Time in India', *Hindustan Times*, 25 March 2020, https://tinyurl.com/2f4hzanw. Accessed on 26 October 2023.
6. 'No. 40-3/2022-DM-I(A)', *Ministry of Home Affairs, Government of India*, https://tinyurl.com/3fzfpe2b. Accessed on 27 October 2023.
7. 'No. 40-3/2020-DM-I(A)', *Ministry of Home Affairs, Government of India*, https://tinyurl.com/2p8nyfva. Accessed on 27 October 2023.
8. 'Explained: Govt Invokes Epidemic Diseases Act, 1897 to Fight Coronavirus; What Is It?', *The Indian Express*, 12 March 2020, https://tinyurl.com/ycybfdw9. Accessed on 26 October 2023.
9. 'The Epidemic Diseases (Amendment) Ordinance, 2020', *PRS Legislative Research*, https://tinyurl.com/3hr6suyu. Accessed on 26 October 2023.
10. Sharma, Neetu Chandra, 'PM Cares Fund to Be Used for Setting up 551 Oxygen Plants', *Mint*, 25 April 2021, https://tinyurl.com/4rtdf7rh. Accessed on 26 October 2023.
11. Singh, Bikash, 'COVID-19 Pandemic: Eight Oxygen Generation Plants Installed in Meghalaya, Nagaland and Tripur', *The Economic Times*, 22 June 2021, https://tinyurl.com/3mtvw8r8. Accessed on 26 October 2023.
12. 'Oxygen Generation Facility Inaugurated at INHS Dhanvantari, Port Blair', *Mint*, 19 July 2021, https://tinyurl.com/3ekderpd. Accessed on 26 October 2023.
13. 'COVID-19: India's Remarkable Story of Ramping-up and Becoming Self-Reliant in Testing', *The Weather Channel*, 21 May 2020, https://tinyurl.com/5r7792z3. Accessed on 26 October 2023.
14. 'Made in India Virus Kits Boost Testing, and Local Industry', *The Economic Times*, 15 October 2023, https://tinyurl.com/2vdtm527. Accessed on 26 October 2023.

15. 'PM Modi Reviews Vaccine Work in Ahmedabad, Hyderabad and Pune', *The Times of India*, 28 November 2020, https://tinyurl.com/4enjnvf6. Accessed on 26 October 2023.
16. 'PM मोदी बोले- कोरोना जैसी आपदा भारत के लिए संदेश और अवसर', *Aaj Tak*, 12 May 2020, https://tinyurl.com/ytt63uwn. Accessed on 27 October 2023.
17. 'India's COVID Fight People Driven; Gets Great Strength from Corona Warriors: PM Modi', *Mint*, 8 October 2020, https://tinyurl.com/ycke6n3f. Accessed on 27 October 2023.
18. 'PM Modi's 9 PM, 9 Minute Appeal | Here's What Will Happen', *India Today*, 5 April 2020, https://tinyurl.com/5y8tx5mj. Accessed on 26 October 2023.
19. Joy, Shemin, 'PM-CARES Fund Got Rs 12,691.82 Crore as Donation in 3 Years', *Deccan Herald*, 8 May 2023, https://tinyurl.com/yxuersx9. Accessed on 26 October 2023.
20. Behera, Pratyuesha, Ipseeta Satpathy, and B. Chandra Mohan Patnaik, 'Medical Assistance and Healthcare Services Facilitated by Self-Help Groups (SHGs) During COVID-19 in India', *Journal of Medicinal and Chemical Sciences,* Volume 5, Issue 4, 2022, 571–580.
21. 'Constitution of the Empowered Groups under the Disaster Management Act 2005', *Ministry of Home Affairs, Government of India*, 29 March 2020, https://tinyurl.com/y5zncety. Accessed on 26 October 2023.
22. Mishra, Mihir, 'COVID-19: Seven Ministries to Set Up Quarantine Facilities', *The Economic Times*, 12 March 2020, https://tinyurl.com/yuj47eec. Accessed on 26 October 2023.
23. 'CoWin in India: The Digital Backbone for the COVID-19 Vaccination Program', *Exemplars in Global Health*, https://tinyurl.com/4nrb5emm. Accessed 26 October 2023.
24. 'Dr. Mansukh Mandaviya Unveils "India's Vaccine Growth Story" at World Book Fair 2023, Pragati Maidan', *Press Information Bureau, Government of India*, 4 March 2023, https://tinyurl.com/4ftuj4p8. Accessed on 26 October 2023.
25. Vanamali, Krishna Veera, 'What Is Vande Bharat Mission?', *Business Standard*, 28 February 2022, https://tinyurl.com/2rckh3sk. Accessed on 26 October 2023.
26. 'Steps Taken by Government to Ameliorate Impact of COVID-19 Pandemic on Indian Economy', *Ministry of Finance, Government of India*, 8 February 2021, https://tinyurl.com/364c4p6n. Accessed on 26 October 2023.
27. 'Programmes on Garib Kalyan Rojgar Abhiyan', *Press Information Bureau,*

Government of India, 5 April 2022, https://tinyurl.com/32z2kf97. Accessed on 26 October 2023.

28. '"Pradhan Mantri Garib Kalyan Package: Insurance Scheme for Health Workers Fighting COVID-19", Extended for a Further Period of 180 Days', *Press Information Bureau, Government of India*, 20 October 2021, https://tinyurl.com/566fb53w. Accessed on 26 October 2023.
29. 'Allocation of Funds to MSMEs', *Press Information Bureau, Government of India*, 9 August 2021, https://tinyurl.com/4wzds5e9. Accessed on 26 October 2023.
30. 'Government Buffered MSME from Bankruptcy with Rs. 3.5 Lakh Crore Loan Support during COVID-19 Pandemic, Says PM', *Press Information Bureau, Government of India*, 15 August 2023, https://tinyurl.com/yzejpzjx. Accessed on 26 October 2023.
31. 'Government Launches Mission COVID Suraksha to Accelerate Indian COVID-19 Vaccine Development', *Press Information Bureau, Government of India,* 29 November 2020, https://tinyurl.com/mrxte5ud. Accessed on 5 October 2023.
32. Pandey, Ashish, 'India Develops First mRNA Vaccine Technology to Fight COVID-19', *India Today,* 14 May 2022, https://tinyurl.com/2cvfsyyx. Accessed on 5 October 2023.
33. 'CoWin in India: The Digital Backbone for the COVID-19 Vaccination Program', *Exemplars in Global Health*, https://tinyurl.com/4nrb5emm. Accessed 26 October 2023.
34. Ibid.
35. 'COVID-19 Contact Tracing App Aarogya Setu Has Alerted 1.4 Lakh Users: Official', *Mint*, 12 May 2020, https://tinyurl.com/55bzyf7e. Accessed on 26 October 2023.